MARCO HEMMERLING   MARKUS GRAF

CASE STUDY HOUSES
DIGITALLY REMASTERED

IMPRINT

Bibliography of the German National Library
The German National Library lists the publication in the German National Bibliography, detailed bibliographical information can be found at http://dnb.ddb.de.

ISBN 978-3-88778-471-3

Marco Hemmerling, Markus Graf
CASE STUDY HOUSES – DIGITALLY REMASTERED

Detmold School of Architecture and Interior Architecture
East-Westphalia University of Applied Sciences

Contributer: Maja Rokohl
Layout and Editorial: Marco Hemmerling
Cover Image: Martin Tintelott
Translation: Ruth M. Deans
Sponsoring: Vectorworks Inc. and ComputerWorks

1. Edition 2016
Spurbuchverlag
96148 Baunach, Germany
info@spurbuch.de
www.spurbuch.de

TABLE OF CONTENTS

THOUSAND OAKS

PASADENA

LOS ANGELES

BEVERLY HILLS

SANTA MONICA

MALIBU

LAX

SOUTH GATE

TORRANCE

ANAHEIM

LONG BEACH

PACIFIC OCEAN

SAN DIEGO

28

15

20A

1

17B 21 17

16A 22

3 16 18A

1950

11

9

8, 18, 20

2

7

25

23

PREFACE UTA POTTGIESSER

A visit to Los Angeles should be compulsory for students of architecture and interior architecture. More than any other place on earth, this city has become an experimental site for modern architectural and spatial visions in the 20th century. Benefitting from a mild climate, the exceptional location on the Pacific Coast and a thriving film industry, Los Angeles has grown rapidly and has become a magnet for people engaged in culture and the arts. This led to the creation of unconventional buildings, usually homes, in spectacular locations as early as 1920; many of them that we know from photographs and advertising and film sets have taken root in our memory. An example is the low-budget Schindler Chase House, built by Rudolph Schindler and Clyde Chase in 1922, and which caused quite a stir with its prefab concrete slabs and sleeping berths made of redwood sets on the roof. Another example is the Ennis house built in 1924 from prefabricated modular concrete blocks by Frank Lloyd Wright and which served, e.g., as film set for "Blade Runner". Another home in this series is Richard Neutra's Lovell House, built in 1929 with a shotcrete covered steel skeleton and which was exhibited as an example of the International Style as early as 1932 in the Museum of Modern Art.

They all became the forerunners of the Case Study Houses that resulted as prototypes from the competition of the Arts & Architecture magazine. The competitions' aim was to combat the housing shortage after WWII with a low-cost, modern home design.

Although the detached residential home may no longer be useful as a model for sustainable urban planning, the Case Study Houses are still an excellent starting point for addressing basic issues of living, and building, and room design, a starting point that provides efficiency with quality.

In his book Marco Hemmerling manages not only to document the valuable didactical approach of the course "Digital Design" at the Detmold School of Architecture and Interior Architecture. Rather, the systematic preparation and visualization of the buildings present a challenge for the development of new and innovative living concepts which contribute towards the solution of the current housing shortage in the metropolises of this world. The students are invited to address the interplay of space, material and construction with the aid of state-of-the-art digital tools for the design of affordable, user-friendly living space.

CASE STUDY HOUSES DIGITALLY REMASTERED

The Case Study House program ranks among the most influential and innovative projects in American architectural history of the post-war period and has not lost any of its fascination until now. Much has already been written about these experimental homes in publications like the monumental retrospective of the Case Study House project (1945 – 1966) published by Taschen or the web-based archive of the Arts and Architecture magazine (www.artsandarchitecture.com) whose editor John Entenza initiated the series in 1945 and documented it in great detail in the monthly issues of the magazine. So why then produce another book on the Case Study Houses?

The present publication interprets the Case Study Houses using the new digital tools that architects now have at their disposal and which make the projects accessible in a wholly different way. While traditional documentation provides floor plans, sections, elevations and perspectives, we are now achieving new insights into the concepts, structure, construction, design and spatial effects of the houses by using 3D models, BIM data and atmospheric visualization as well as advanced image processing. It is even possible to download 3D models of some of the houses and try out novel approaches to individual projects.

The idea for this book is a further development of an academic project with first-year Bachelor students at the Detmold School of Architecture and Interior Architecture.

The theoretical engagement with the Case Study Houses during the "Digital Design" course was an ideal basis for a first introduction to computer-aided design and planning tools. The modular and easily readable system design on which the houses are constructed and the building geometries which tend to be fairly simple, facilitate access to the design concept and first steps with CAD software for the students. In the seminar students were taught digital methods for 2D plan creation, 3D modelling, visualization, image processing and layout design, as well as the reflection on and interpretation of the various designs of the case study houses. This book demonstrates step by step the creation process, and the result of the students' work give an idea of the applied modelling and visualization techniques.

Above all, the book should serve as an inspiration for new architectural ideas and promote the use of digital technologies in the design, visualization and realization of such concepts in creative and innovative ways.

The enjoyment of experimenting and the fascination for all that is new should, however, always be driven by the benefit and the user, as we can learn from the Case Study Houses. John Entenza defined the essential prerequisites for successful architecture already when he wrote: „Let's begin with man, with respect, compassion and love for the individual—or we'll never get anywhere."

THE CASE STUDY HOUSE PROGRAM 1945-1966

From Ray and Charles Eames and Pierre Koenig's legendary light steel constructions to the visionary villas of John Lautner and the first daring architectural projects of Frank O. Gehry, Eric Owen Moss and Thomas Mayne – in California any number of these architecturally unique private homes can be found. In fact, the Case Study houses initiated by Arts & Architecture (A&A) in 1945 made California the cradle of experimental, modern architecture in the post-war era. John Entenza, publisher and editor-in-chief of the magazine and ardent advocate of modernity was the major driving force behind the project.

The ambitious program that lasted well into the middle of the 1960s represents an extraordinary and innovative episode in the history of building and strongly influenced the development of American and international architecture. The designs of renowned avant-garde architects such as Richard Neutra, Craig Ellwood, Raphael Soriano and Eero Saarinen were focused on low-cost houses that were simple and quick to erect, and succeeded in coming up with unique houses that were to redefine the entire concept of modern living.

In line with industrial mass production, the aim was to prefabricate houses to the extent that they could be built as fast as possible. Notwithstanding the low building costs, the houses were expected to satisfy the demands of prosperous Americans of the post-war boom.

The popular trend in line with the Bauhaus concept also went for open living space and functional structures.

A&A was used to promote the building of the houses by presenting in each monthly issue selected homes with details of construction and designs. This gave welcome exposure to the architects most of which were still young but also served to promote the contractors and manufacturers. The clients received the necessary materials at a substantially reduced price but had to open their house as showcases for inspection. Of the 36 houses initially designed only 25 were actually built but most of these still exist today. The first six were finished in 1948 and attracted more than 350,000 visitors. Most of the Case Study Houses were set up in the greater Los Angeles area, a few also in the San Francisco area and one in Phoenix.

From the architectural tristesse of Los Angeles which was so aptly describes by Mike Davis in his critical book "City of Quartz" these architectural islands stand out impressively and serve as reference for innovative, modern and at the same time people-focused architecture of desire. The effectively staged photos by Julius Shulman contributed not least to the aestheticization of these homes and made them to what they are to this day – icons of modern architecture

ARTS & ARCHITECTURE

CSH VS. CAD

CSH VS. CAD

The Case Study Houses are representative of the innovative and creative use of the technical possibilities of their time and they appear amazingly modern even today. The combination of industrial prefabrication and experimental styles of living were tested in these visionary prototypes; new technology and methods act as driving forces for new thoughts. Today we are once more in the middle of a new wave of technologisation. Computer Aided Design (CAD), digital planning and building, building information modelling, Industry 4.0, the Internet of Things and Big Data – all these stand for this shift. The translation of planning and production approaches of those days with the methods at our disposal today allows not only the reflection on the built environment but opens a wide vista into the future with new ideas of designing, planning and building.

A major advantage of using digital technology is the multiple ways in which individual computer-aided applications can be linked. The necessary foundation of such strategies is the development of a comprehensive three-dimensional model that can be developed and advanced through progressive planning processes. From this model are derived all relevant later presentations in form of technical drawings, atmospheric visualization, analytical simulation and machine-readable fabrication data for planning and construction.

The illustrations of the Case Study Houses in the following chapter were developed with such a model-based approach. Floor plan and elevations are extracted from the consistent 3D model of the house which incorporates all relevant planning data.

All digital models are available for download from:
www.vectorworks.de/case-study-houses

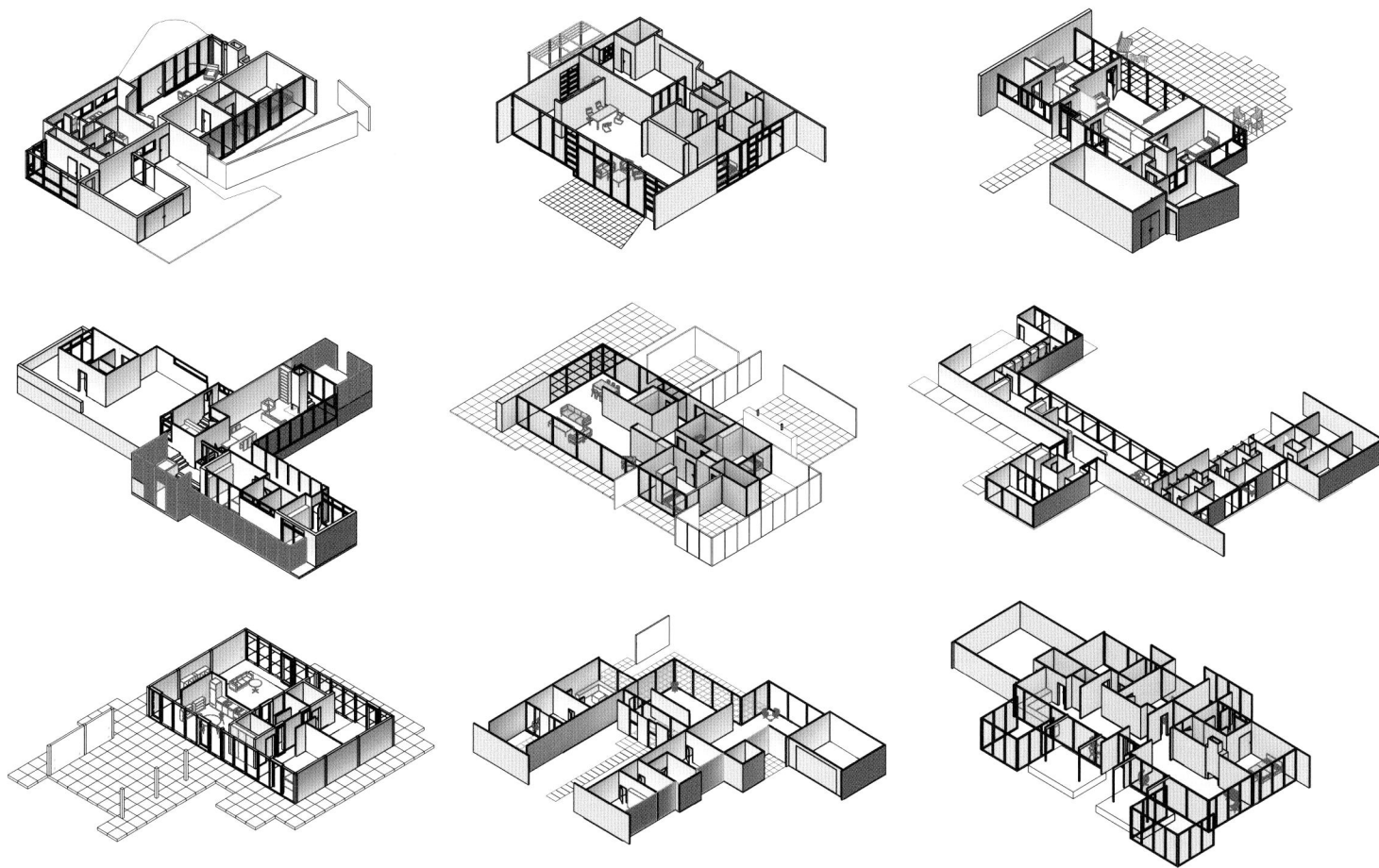

CSH #7

1945-48
6236 NORTH DEERFIELD, SAN GABRIEL
ARCHITECT: THORNTON ABELL

This house built in the east of Los Angeles in 1948 differs substantially from its first published draft versions. Its original owner was an employee of a roofing contractor who was involved in many of the Case Study Houses. A family room that the architect Thornton Abell had positioned between the kitchen and the living room could be used flexibly for various activities. The walls between these rooms could be pushed aside so that the family had one big room at their disposal, as and when needed. Outer spaces, terraces and patios were also laid out in accordance with the principle of functional structuring; private bedrooms were separated from the public area by unbroken masonry walls and faced towards the patio. The supporting structure of the house is mainly constructed of lightweight concrete blocks and plywood walls.

17

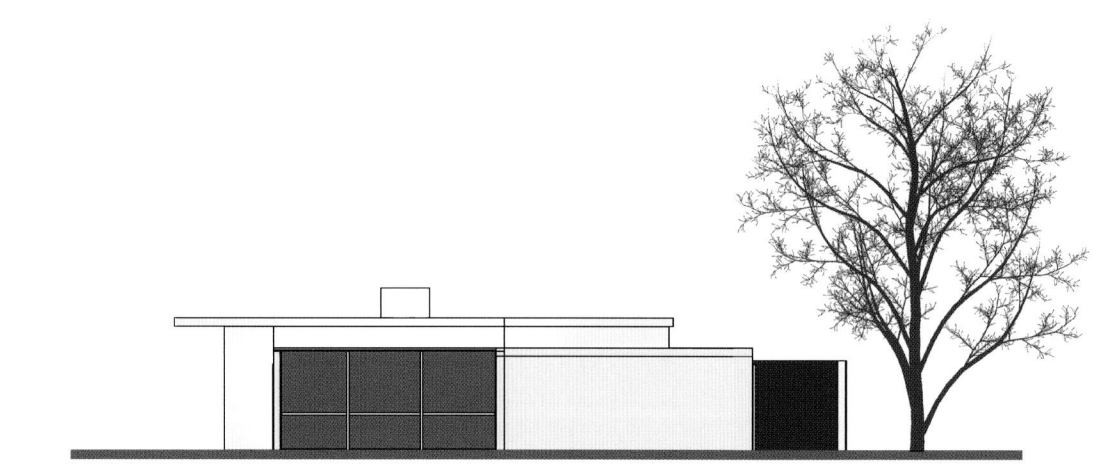

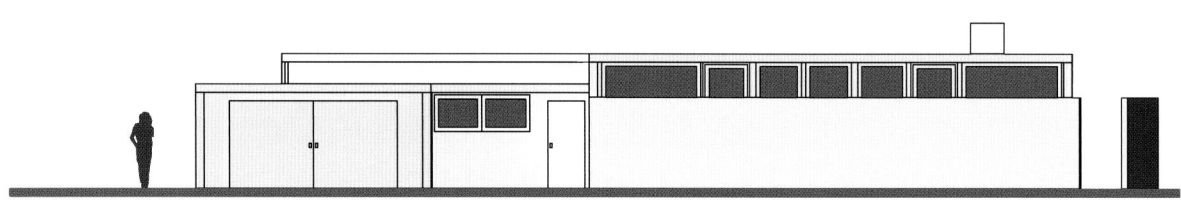

18

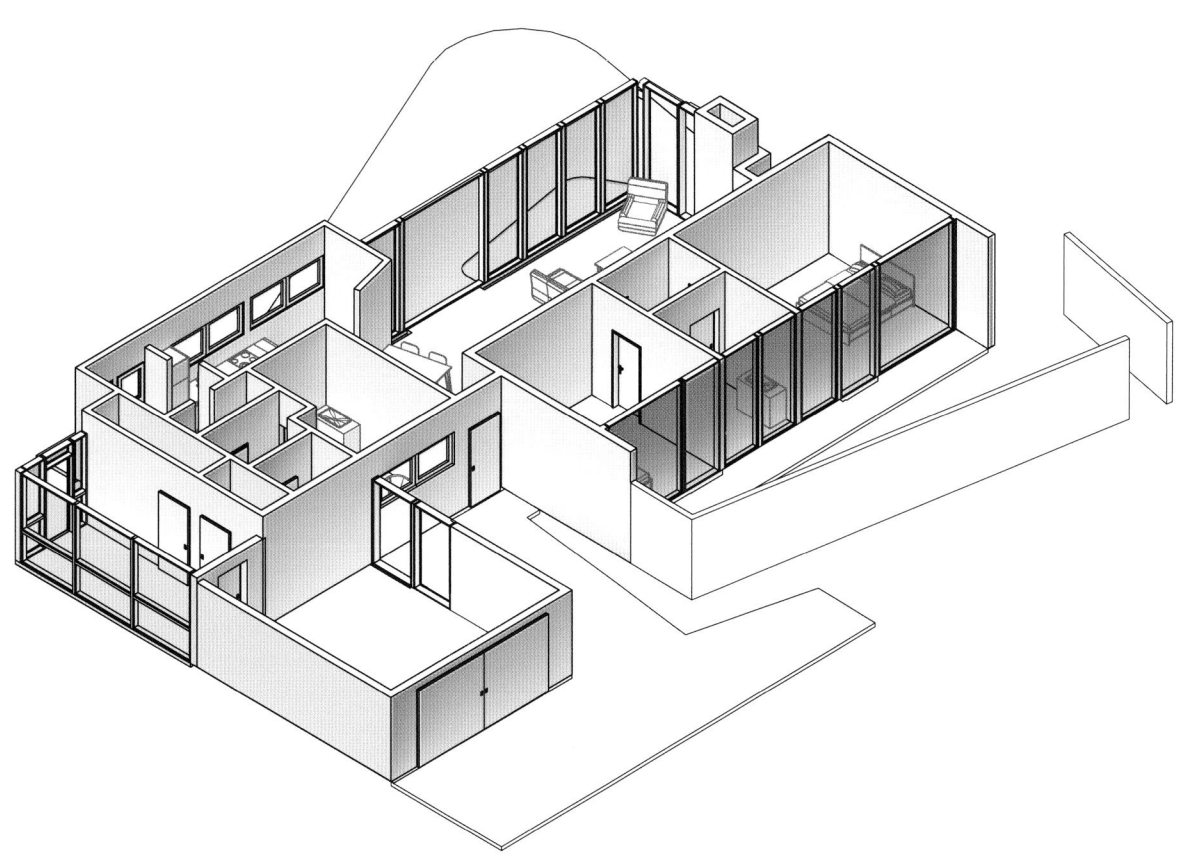

CSH #9 ENTENZA HOUSE

1945-1949
205 CHAUTAUQUA BOULEVARD, PACIFIC PALISADES
ARCHITECTS: CHARLES EAMES AND EERO SAARINEN

The home of the initiator of the CSH series and editor of the magazine Arts and Architecture, John Entenza shared a building site with Charles and Ray Eames, the owners of CSH #8, a two storey house built in the same year. Critics called the two houses "technological twins but architectural contrasts". The Entenza House combines a strict construction of steel and glass with inner rooms where the constructive elements are hidden by plastered walls and wood paneling. The simple rectangular layout of the house – one of the first steel frame constructions of the Show House program – allowed for a flexible room layout. The design of the public rooms is notably more generous than that of the private rooms. The façade, oriented towards the west, is completely glazed and thereby opens the inner space to the terraces, the garden and beyond, right up to the ocean.

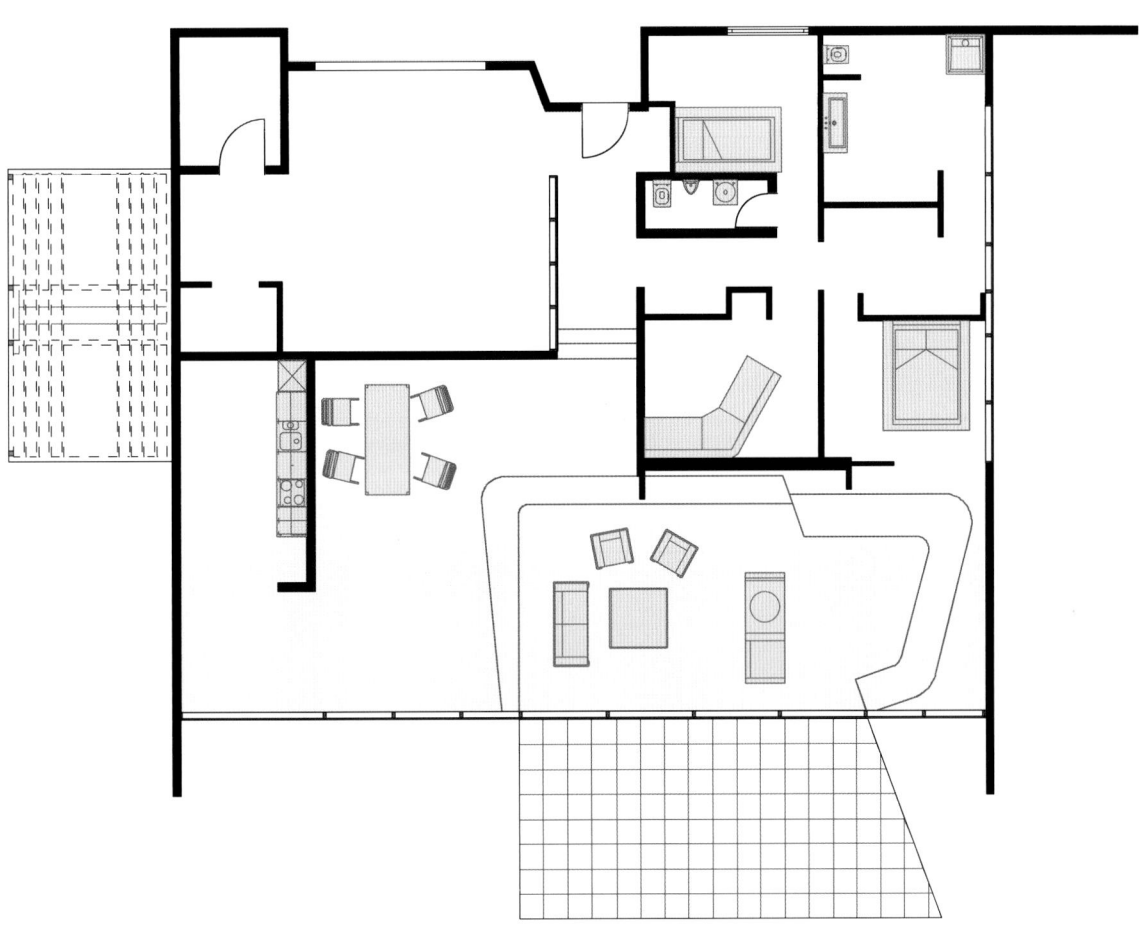

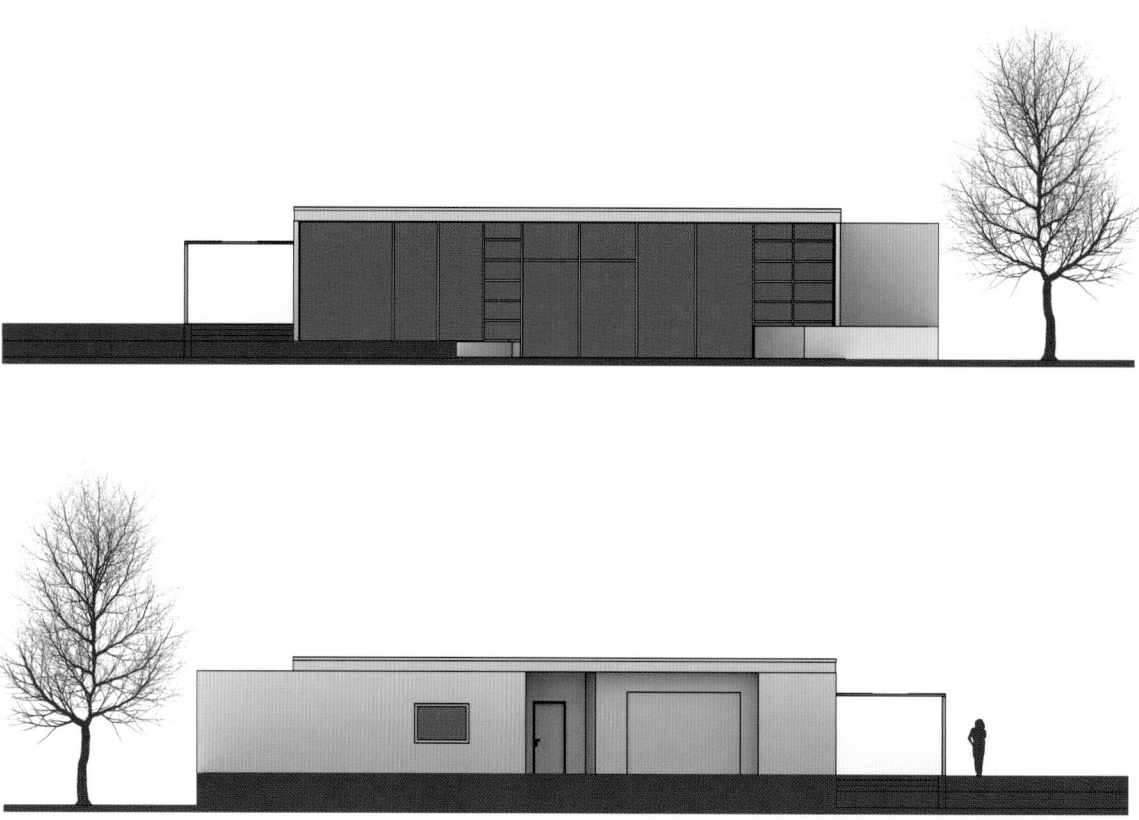

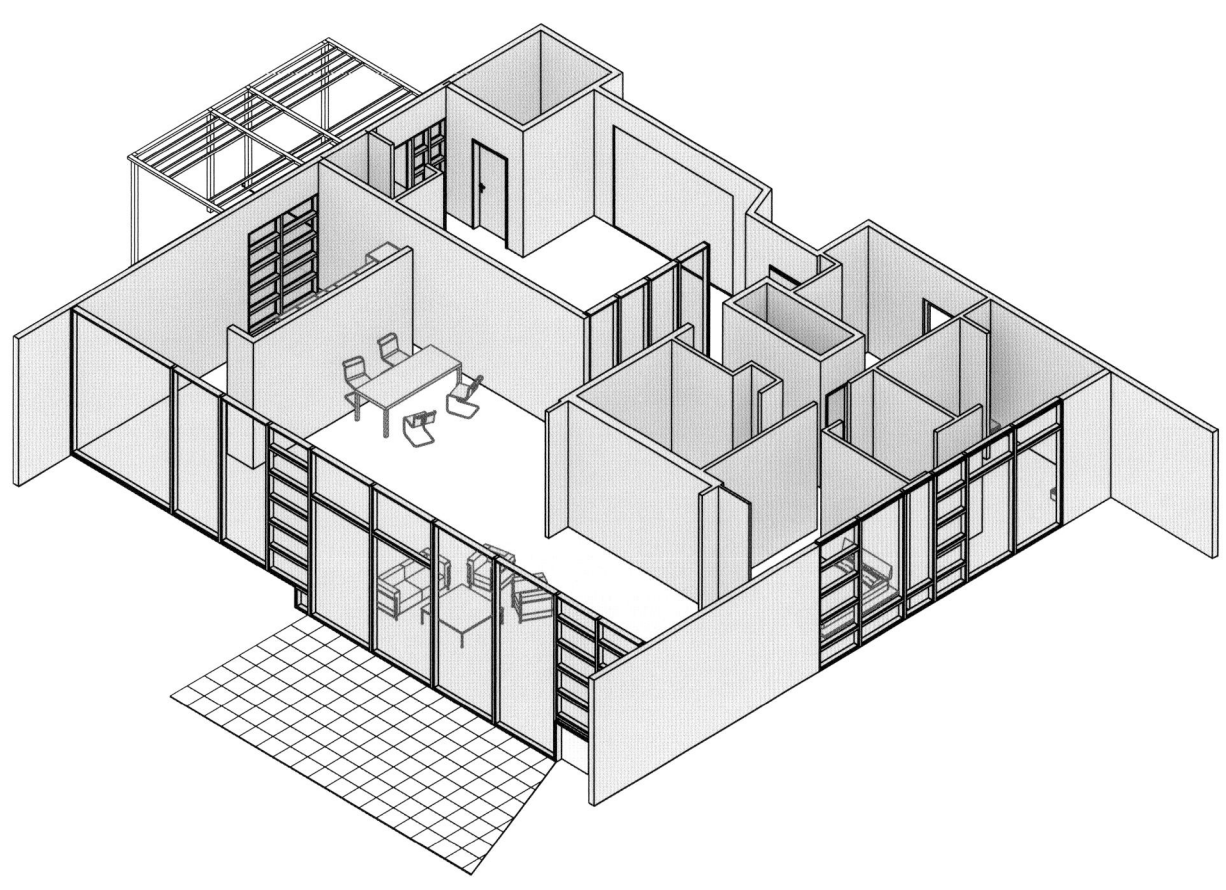

CSH #11

1945-1946
540 SOUTH BARRINGTON AVENUE, LOS ANGELES
ARCHITECT: JULIUS RALPH DAVIDSON

This house in the west of Los Angeles is the first that was completed as a show house in the course of the program. The owner was the advertising manager of the magazine Arts & Architecture and his family. Though of moderate design and simple construction the architect and the building contractor had to cope with a number of challenges presented by the shortage of materials after the war which led to delays in the completion of the house. Nevertheless, this first Case Study House presented a successful example of a compact, reasonably-priced house with a well-laid out floor plan. The structure consists of a wooden framework with wood paneling and glass walls. After completion, the house was opened to the public as part of the advertising campaign created for the Case Study Houses. More than 55,000 people visited the house and thereby created the desired publicity for the program.

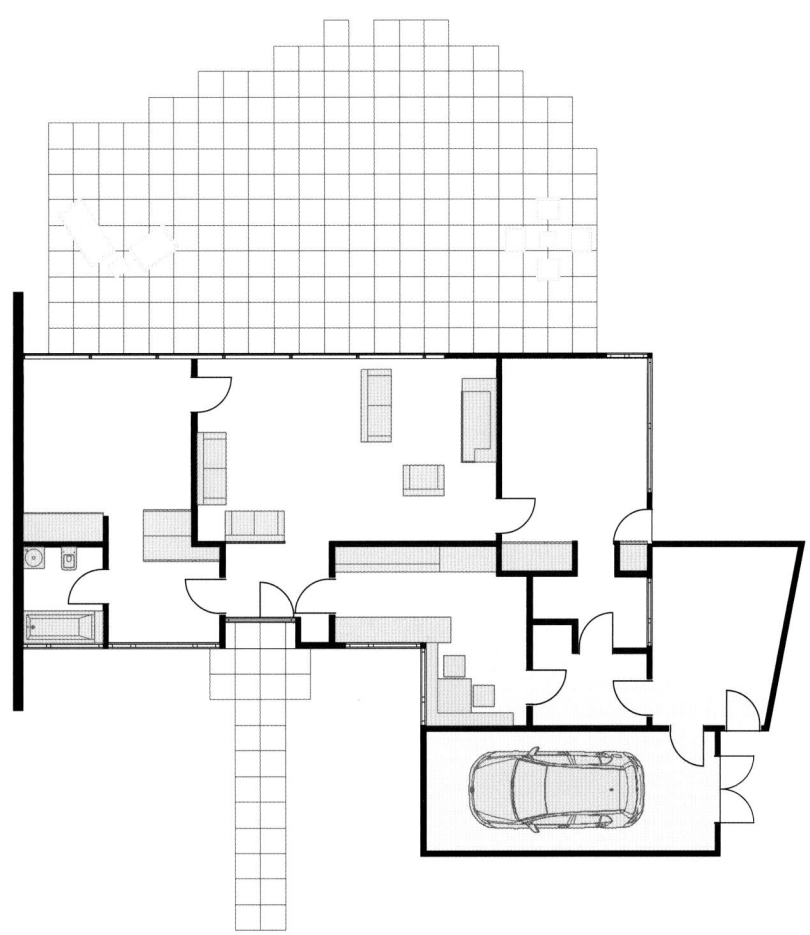

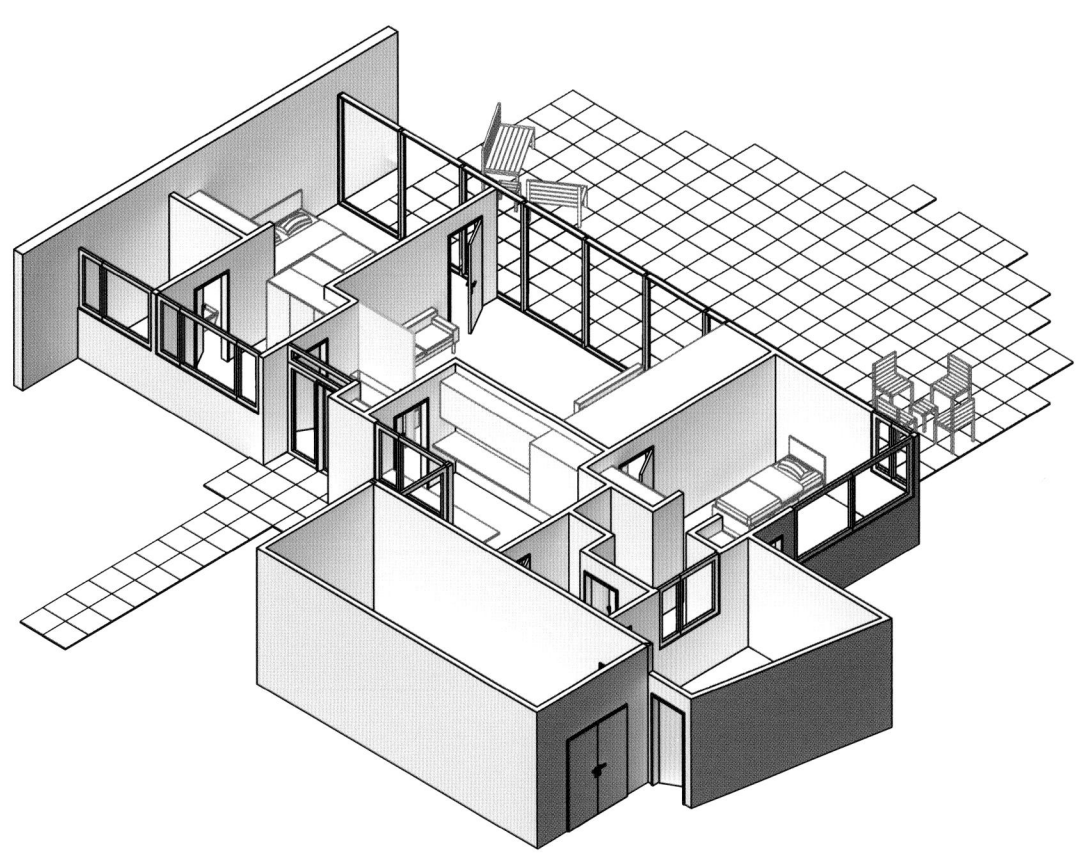

CSH #16A

1952-1953
1811 BEL AIR ROAD, BEL AIR
ARCHITECT: CRAIG ELLWOOD

This is the first of three houses designed by Craig Ellwood for the program. Ellwood who trained as a civil engineer and who started his career working for a construction company used mainly industrial materials and manufacturing techniques for this rather factual design. A combination of steel, glass and concrete determines the rational character of the house. The elegant detailed solutions and the partially detached massive translucent and transparent walls manage to create a lightness that seemingly allows outer and inner spaces to blend into each other. The garden patio, the terrace and the barbecue area are part of the spatial overall composition and serve as an extension to the inner functions of the house. The long cantilevered roofs which cover nearly double the area of the floorplan enhance this effect and additionally offer an effective protection from the California sunshine.

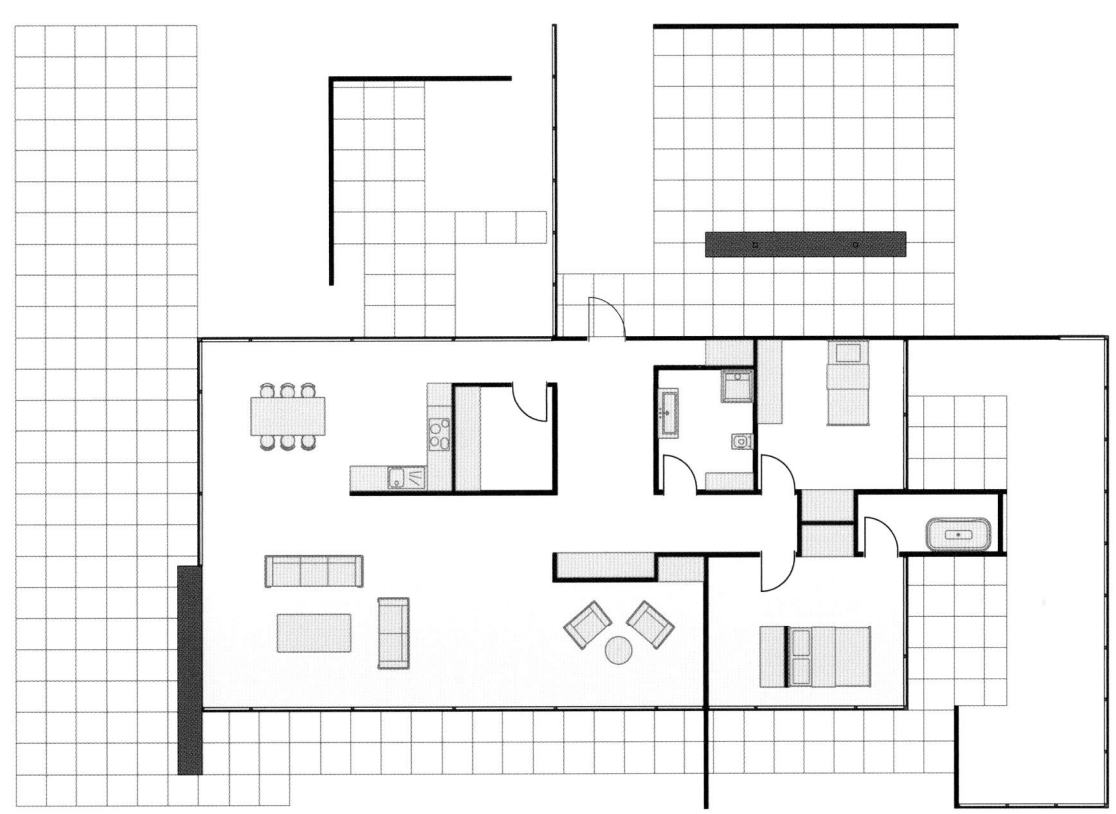

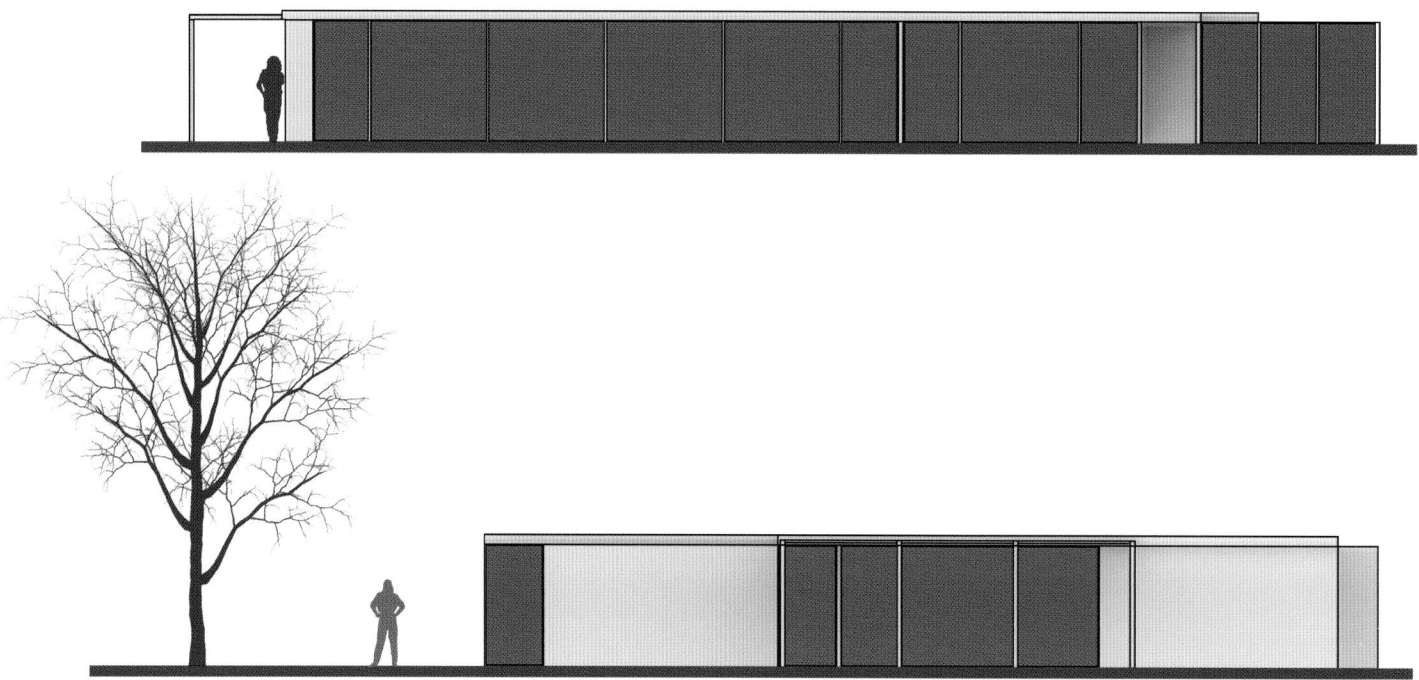

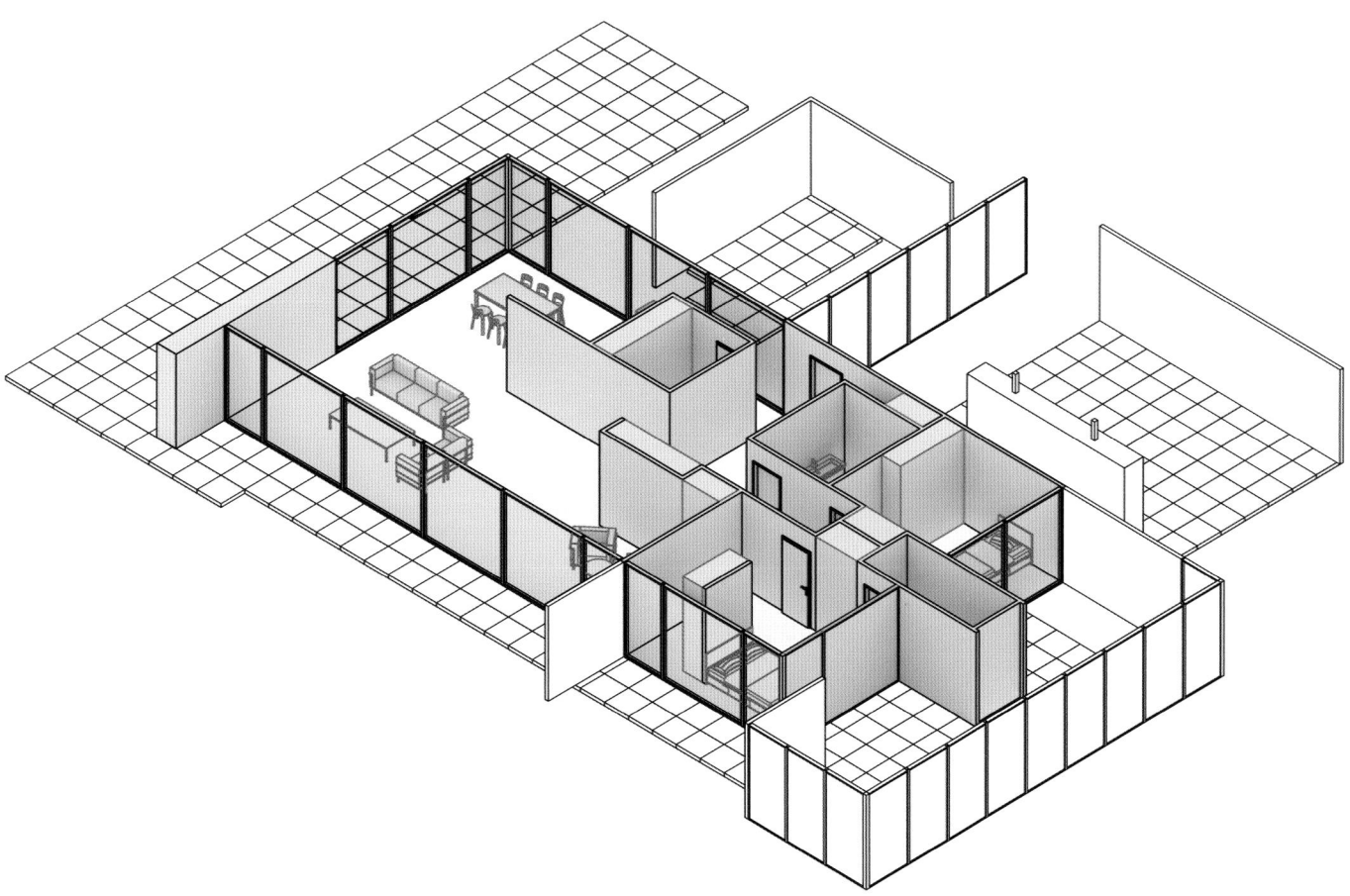

CSH #17B

1954-1955
9554 HIDDEN VALLEY ROAD, BEVERLY HILLS
ARCHITECT: CRAIG ELLWOOD

This house is not only substantially larger but with its swimming pool, tennis court and many technical features it is also considerably more luxuriously equipped than all previously built Case Study Houses. In this spacious house on a U-shaped floorplan all bedrooms are in a wing sitting at right-angles to the central section with dining room, kitchen and living area. The ancillary rooms and the carport are located in the third wing opposite. From all the rooms, the terrace and the adjoining swimming pool can be accessed through sliding glass doors. Same as he had already done in his first show house of the series, Craig Ellwood also used a visible steel frame construction here with transparent and translucent glass partition walls and brick infill. Only a few years later, new owners had the house converted in a pseudo-classicistic style and thereby, sadly, rendering it completely unrecognizable as a Case Study House.

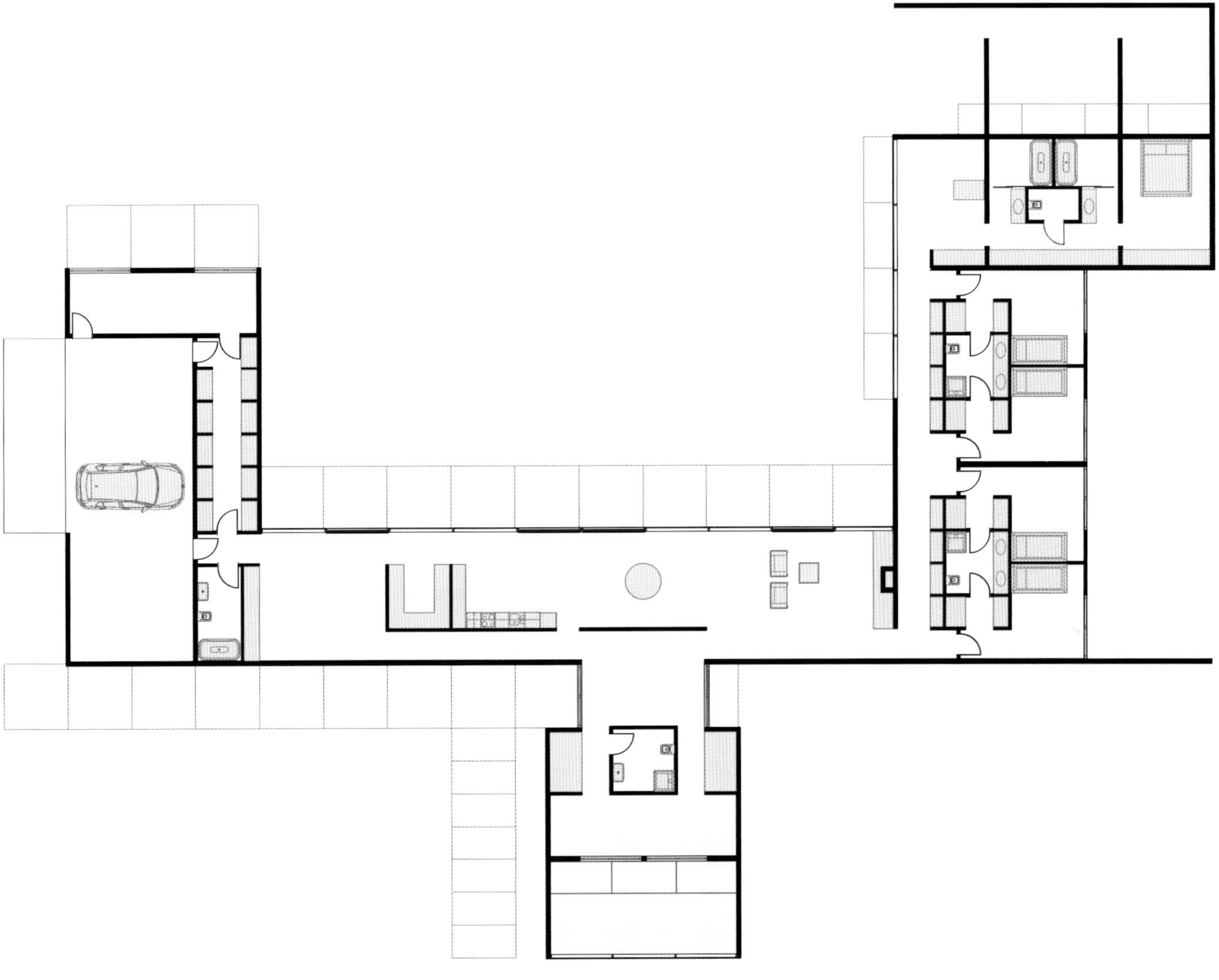

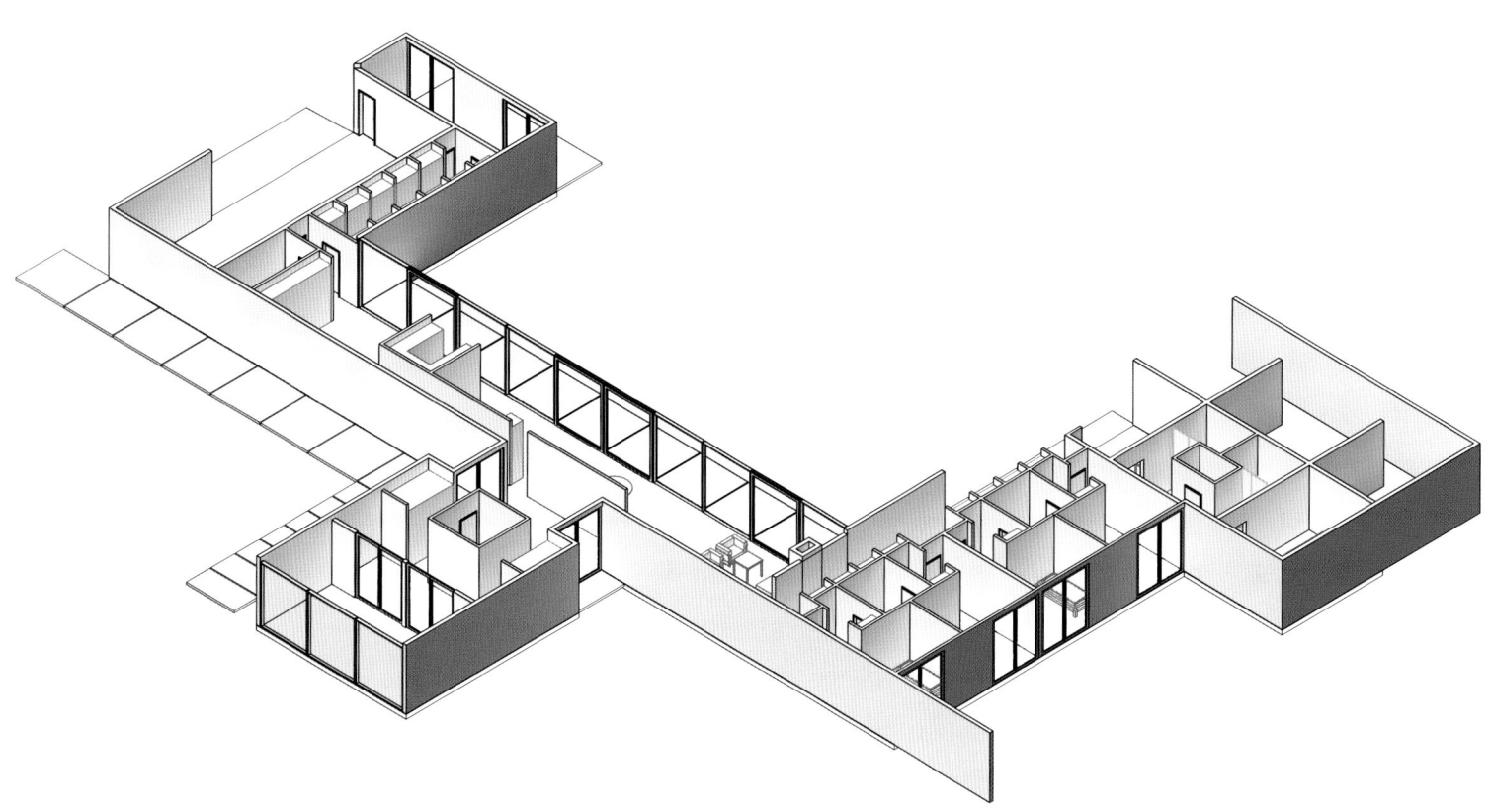

CSH #21

1958
9038 WONDERLAND PARK AVENUE, LOS ANGELES
ARCHITECT: PIERRE KOENIG

This single storey L-shaped building was constructed in a side valley of the Hollywood Hills for a childless couple and is defined by its innovative prefabrication, its assembly and the perfect detail of its steel construction. An additional architectural innovation was the building's technology housed at the core of the building with bathroom and warm water treatment plant, which also served as a division between the living area and the bedrooms. The building consists of a living section oriented towards the east-west and a car port on the northern side which is seamlessly integrated in the building. The northern and the western facades are glazed down to the ground. White façade panels made of metal shield the house against the street. The house was renovated completely in the middle of the 1990s, based on the original plan, including the furniture which had been specifically designed by Pierre Koenig for the project.

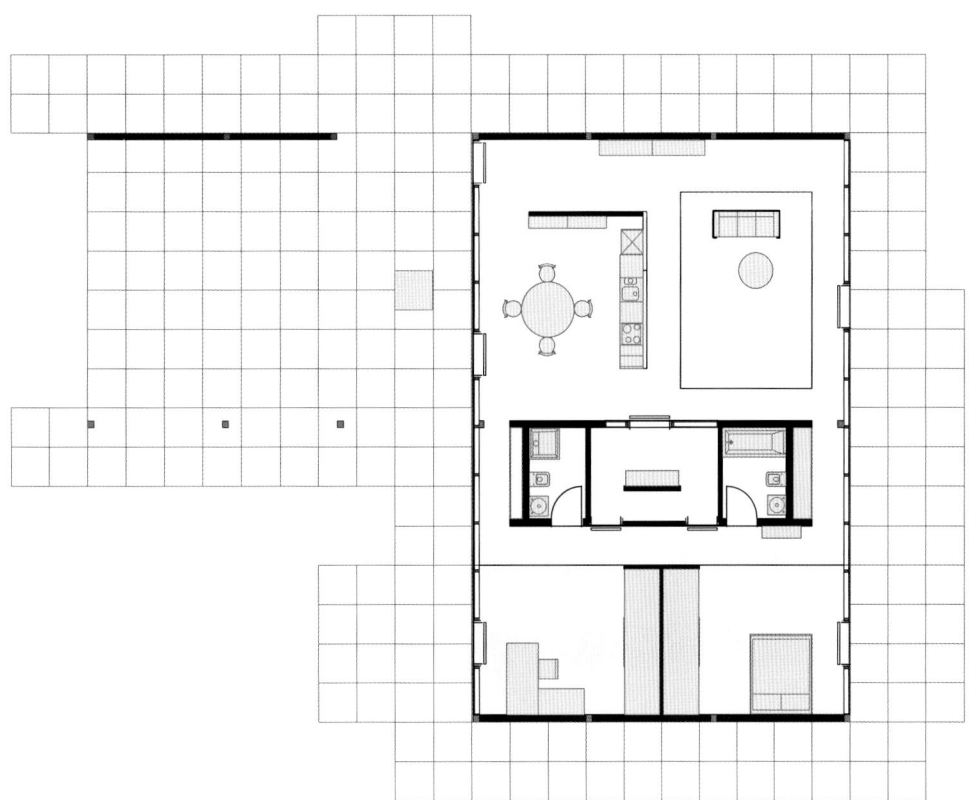

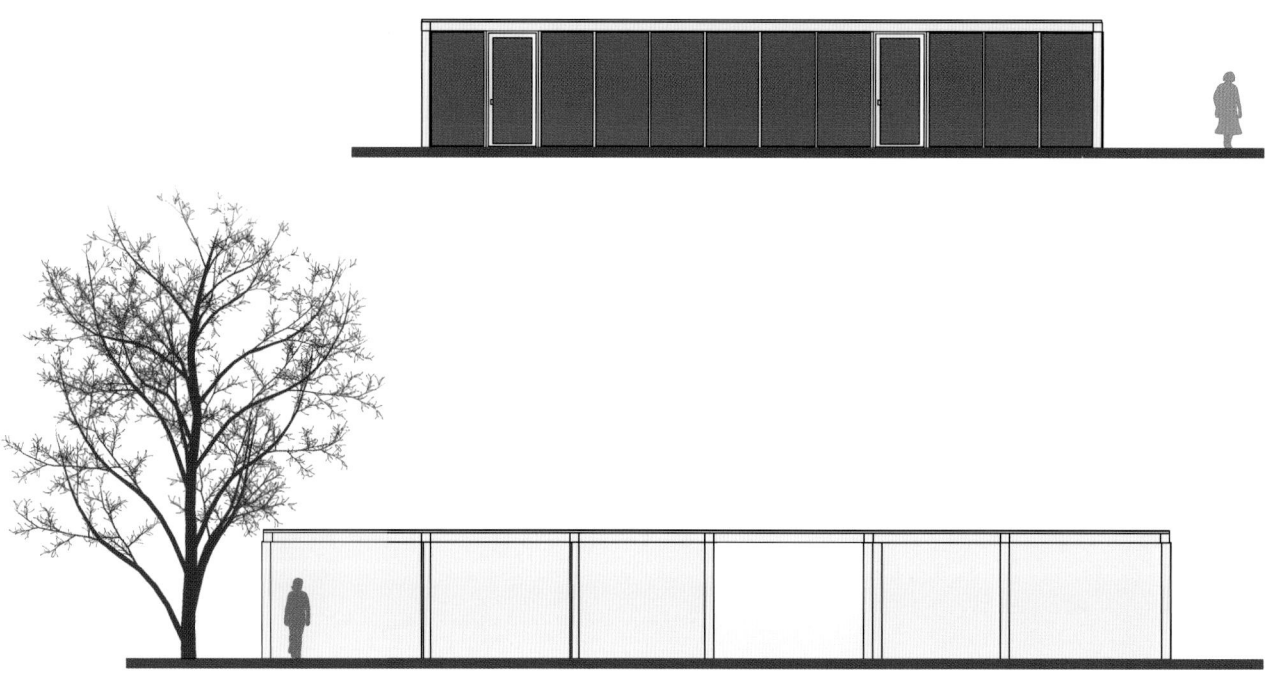

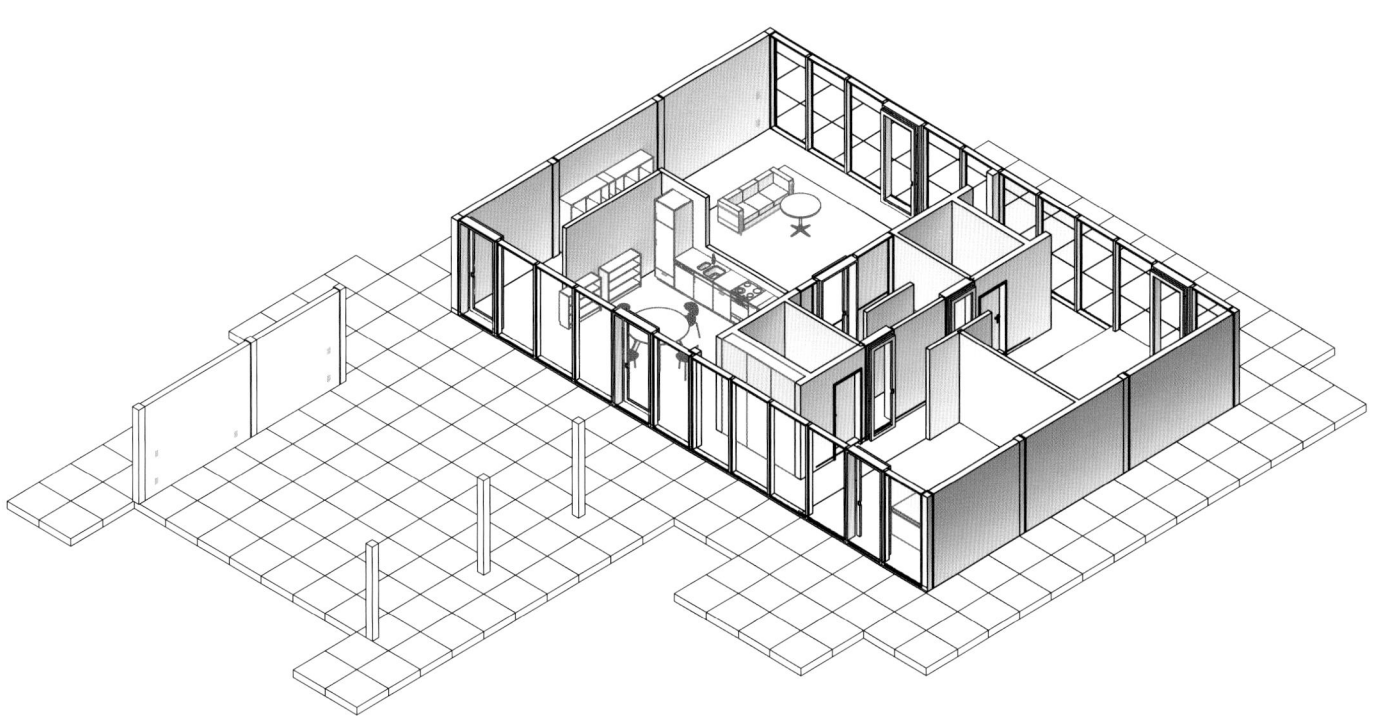

CSH #23A TRIAD HOUSES

1959–1960
RUE DE ANNE, LA JOLLA
ARCHITECTS: KILLINGSWORTH, BRADY & SMITH

The Case Study House Project #23 - also known as the Triad - is made up of three houses on a hillside property, cleverly set in relation to one another. The buildings A, B and C differ in size, room division and façade as well as in the way the outer spaces are designed and provide living space for different lifestyles. The building materials that were used and the technical features as well as the wooden frame construction and the materials for the inner wall claddings and the floors are, however, identical. House A, the largest of the Triad buildings lies below the other two dwellings and is based on a U-shaped floorplan. Unusual here is the additional family room next to the living room and the kitchen. The central entrance area is reached via a bridge-type access made of concrete slabs across a reflecting pond. The façade made of Redwood panels and the room-high glazing focus cleverly on the private and the public areas of the house so that certain areas are screened off from inquisitive looks from the outside but inner rooms still have the view of the extensive outside areas.

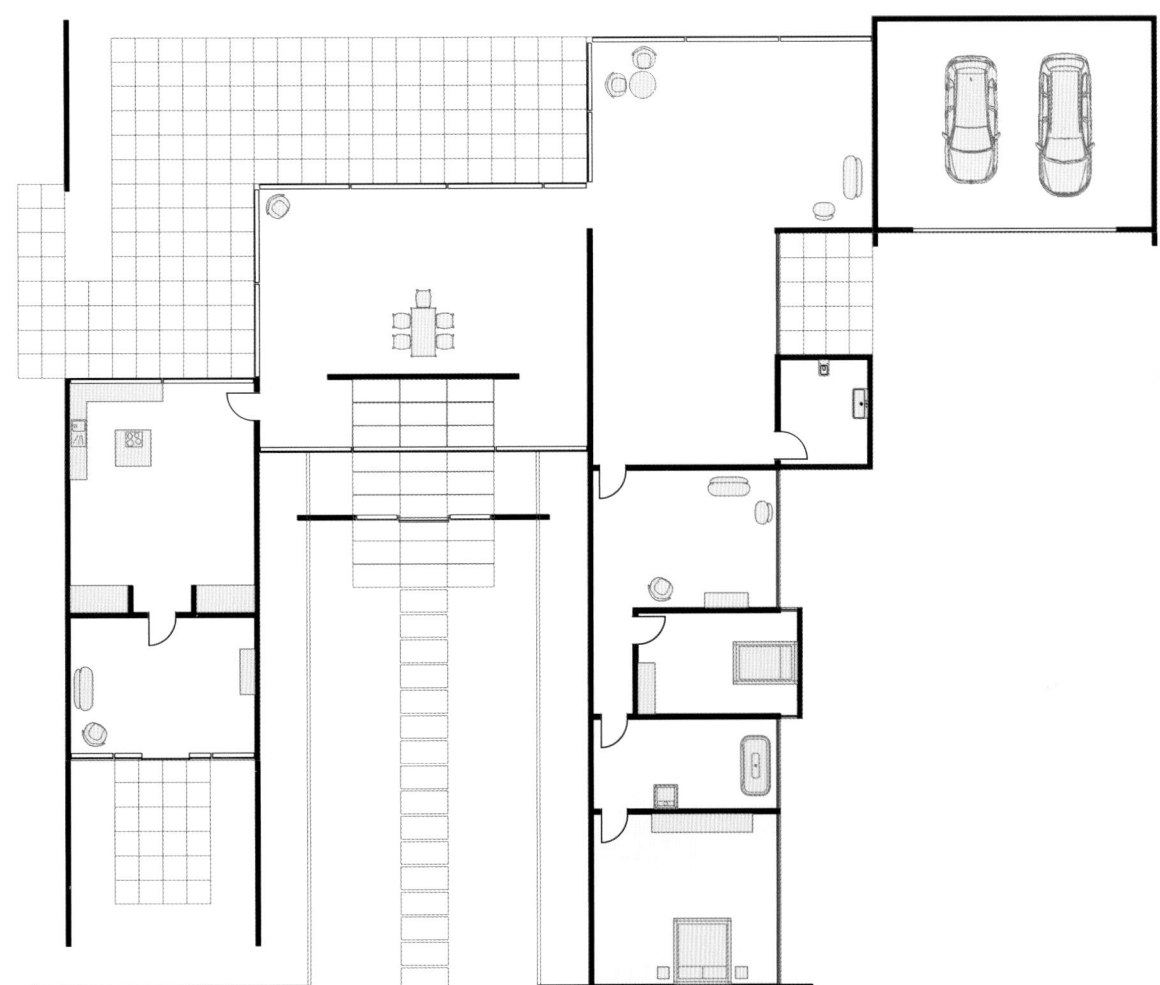

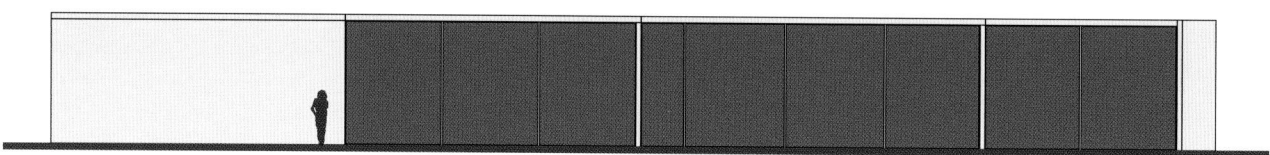

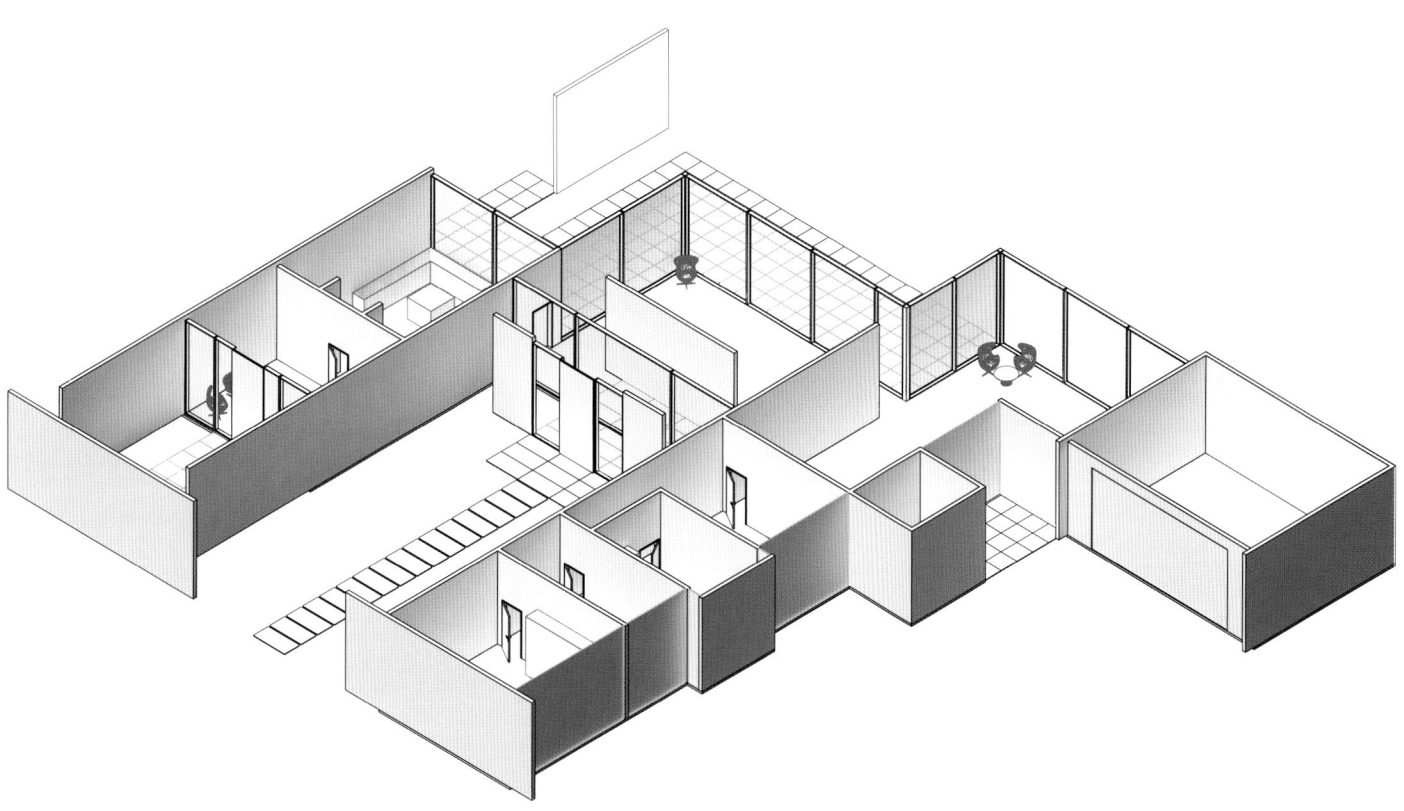

CSH MAKING OF

CSH MAKING OF

It is not only the architects' working practices that have become greatly influenced by the use of digital tools in the past decades but also the multitude of architectural design options and the resulting presentation and perception of architecture. The Bachelor course "Digital Design" aimed therefore at providing students with a holistic competence in the application of digital methods in design and planning processes. In parallel with practical applications in our seminars, a lecture series introduced the theoretical context and kept a critical and constructive eye on the influence of digital technologies in architecture.

The 3D models of the Case Study Houses were successively developed and produced by the students in modular-structured seminars, leading from the foundations to the erection of space-creating walls with windows and doors and roof constructions right through to the interior furnishing. The 3D model was carried forward with a visualization program which covered the positioning of natural and artificial daylight sources and finally transferred into renderings. With digital image processing the renderings were optimized in terms of contrast, brightness and color adjustment and completed with photomontage of persons and suitable items. As a last step all images produced in the process (floor plan, section, elevation, detail, 3D model, visualization, graphics and typography) were brought together in a layout design.

The following example uses Pierre Koenig's Case Study House #22 which is very likely the best known house from the series and demonstrates the individual steps and thereby offers a visual impression of the work process described above.

Under the heading "CSH- best of" selected undergraduate student projects have been collated; which show great variety in their individual interpretations of diverse Case Study Houses.

3D-MODELLING FOUNDATION

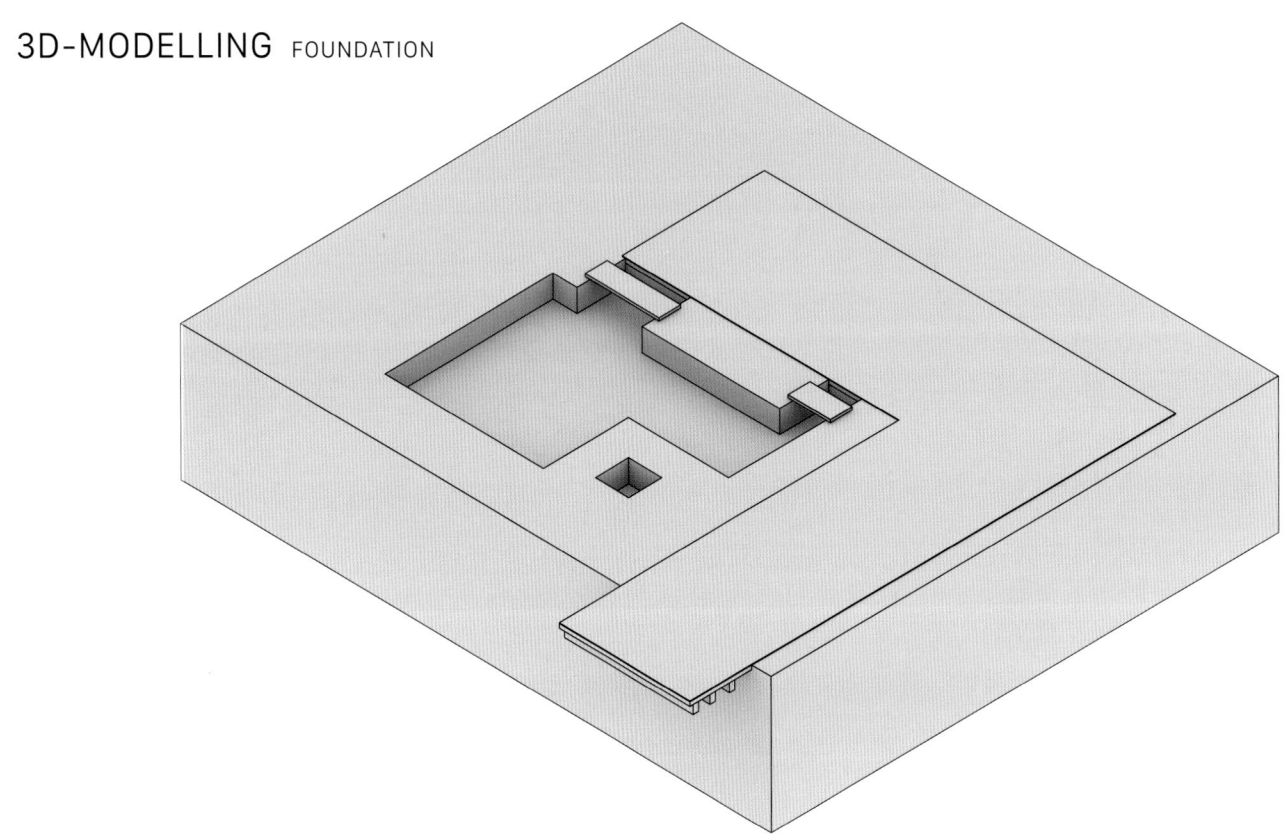

3D-MODELLING WALLS

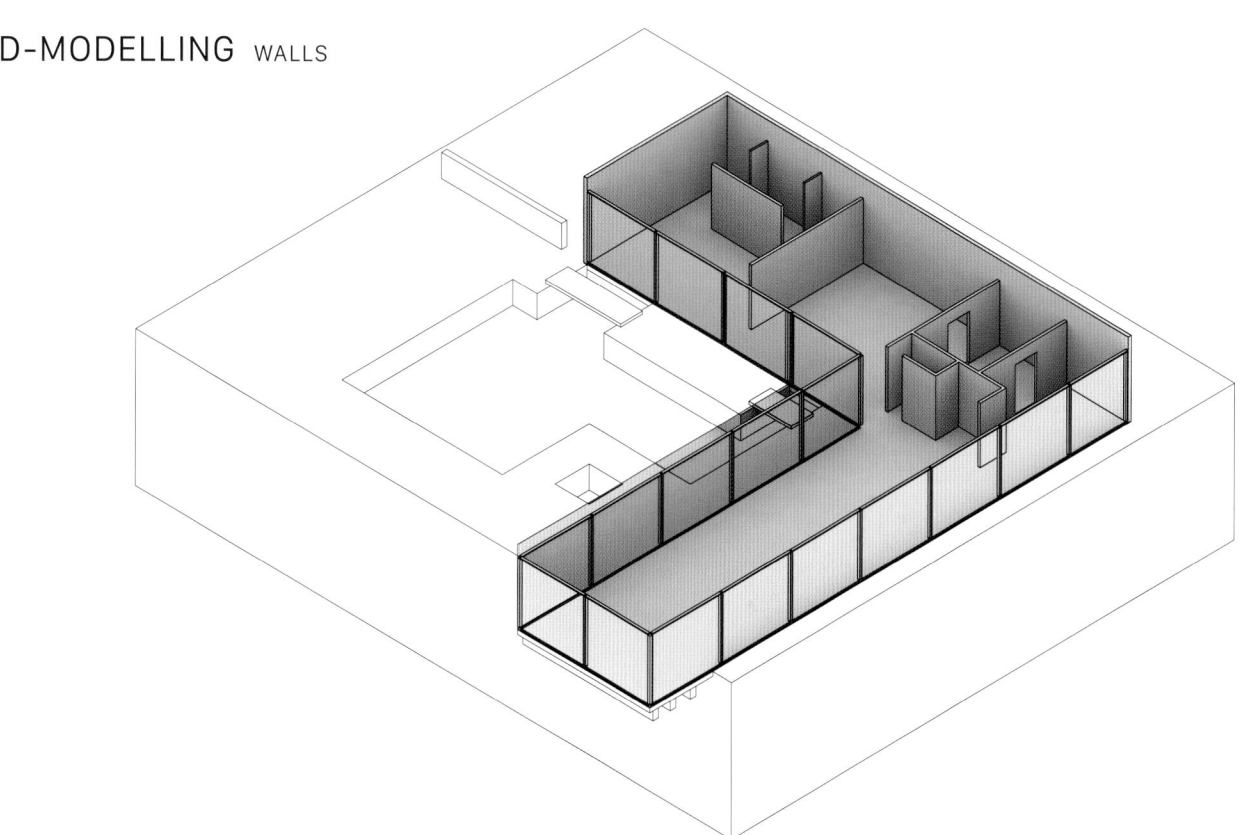

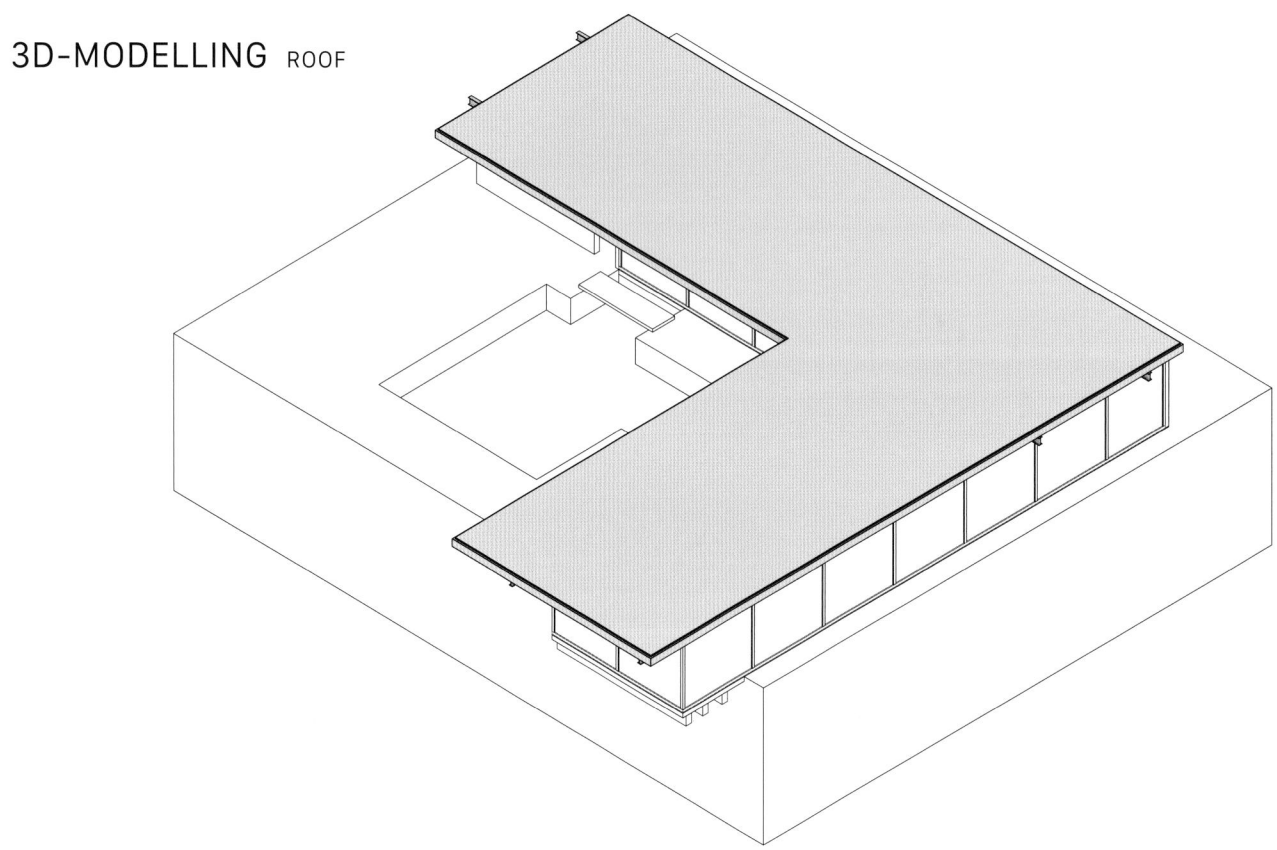

3D-MODELLING FURNITURE

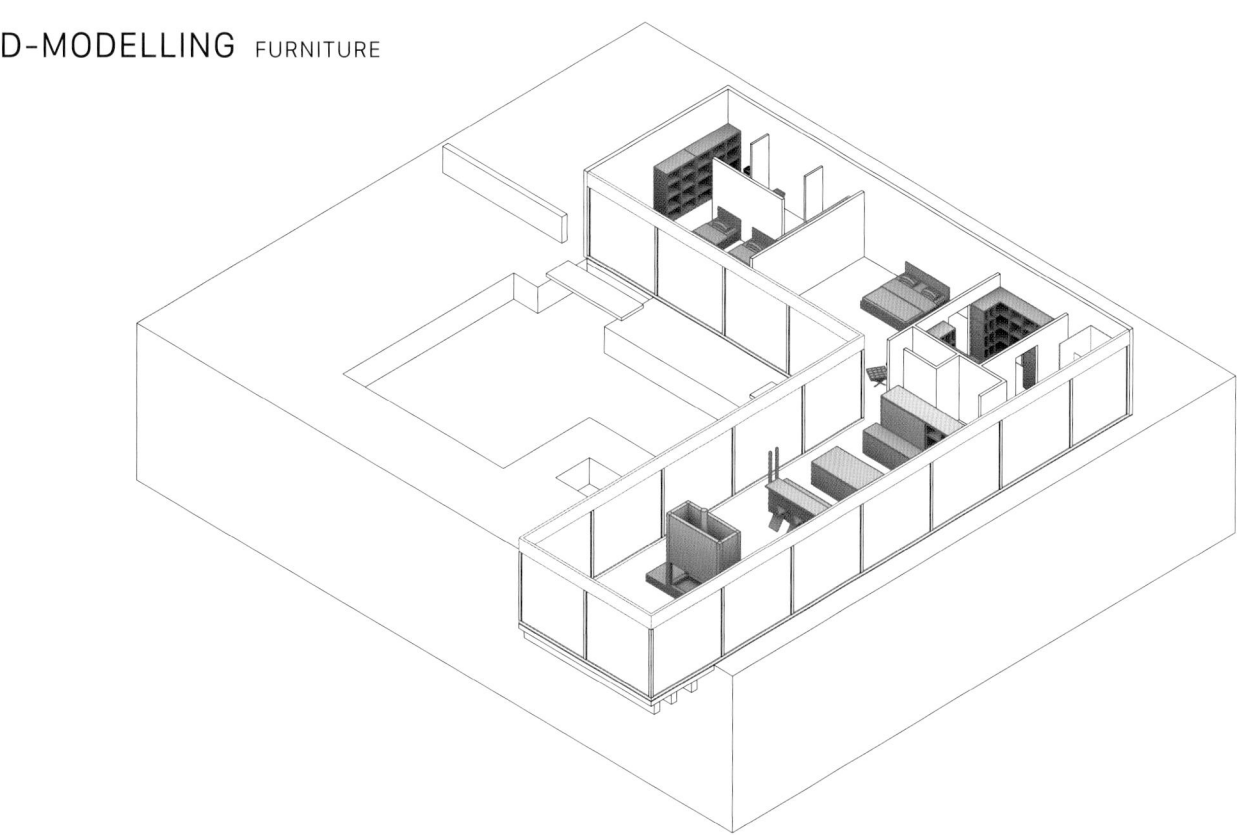

VISUALIZATION MATERIAL

IMAGE PROCESSING

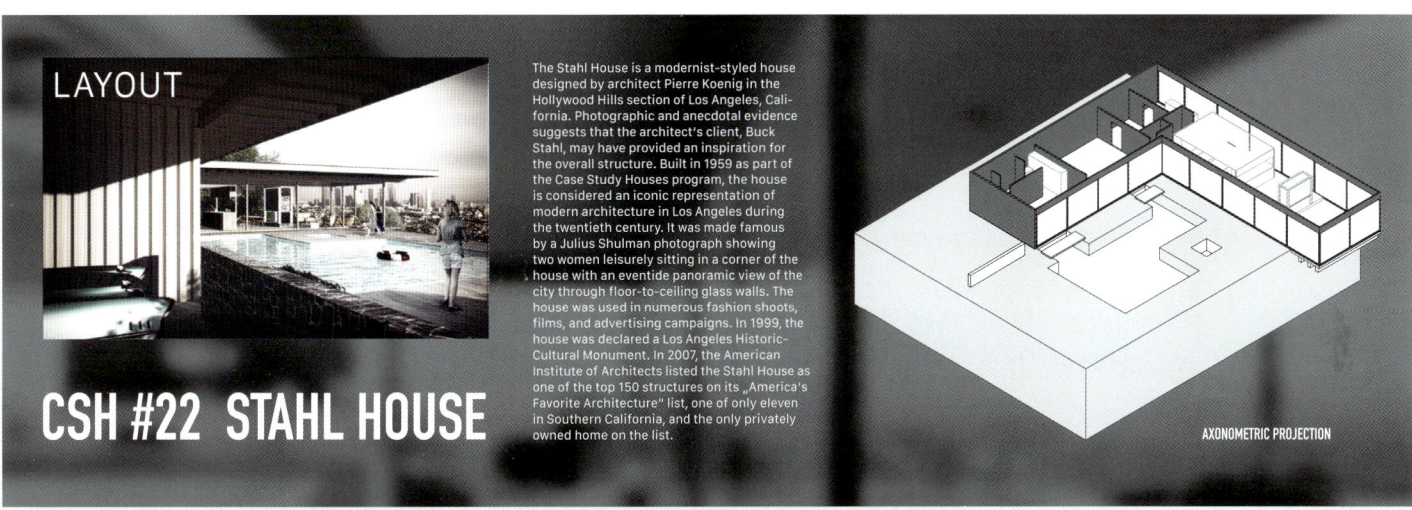

LAYOUT

CSH #22 STAHL HOUSE

The Stahl House is a modernist-styled house designed by architect Pierre Koenig in the Hollywood Hills section of Los Angeles, California. Photographic and anecdotal evidence suggests that the architect's client, Buck Stahl, may have provided an inspiration for the overall structure. Built in 1959 as part of the Case Study Houses program, the house is considered an iconic representation of modern architecture in Los Angeles during the twentieth century. It was made famous by a Julius Shulman photograph showing two women leisurely sitting in a corner of the house with an eventide panoramic view of the city through floor-to-ceiling glass walls. The house was used in numerous fashion shoots, films, and advertising campaigns. In 1999, the house was declared a Los Angeles Historic-Cultural Monument. In 2007, the American Institute of Architects listed the Stahl House as one of the top 150 structures on its „America's Favorite Architecture" list, one of only eleven in Southern California, and the only privately owned home on the list.

AXONOMETRIC PROJECTION

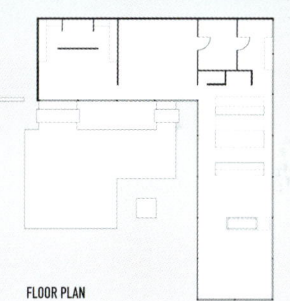

FLOOR PLAN

CSH #22 STAHL HOUSE

1959-1960
1635 WOODS DRIVE, LOS ANGELES
ARCHITECT: PIERRE KOENIG

The Stahl House is most likely the best known and the most radical of the Case Study House program. The L-shaped building centered around a rectangular swimming pool was erected on a slope which was considered unsuitable for building. The private rooms are accommodated in the wing transverse to the slope, while the open living area in the second wing with built-in kitchen furniture and chimney form a cantilever above the slope. This southern part of the building is glazed from bottom to the steel roof and so offers a spectacular view across the city from all its rooms. That Case Study House #22 became the most famous example of the series, the architect owes to the direction of photographer Julius Shulman. No one else managed to provide such an effective visual statement of the lifestyle of this Californian experiment. There are only few photos of 20th century buildings with the cult value of the photos of Pierre Koenig's house that seems to float above the nightlights of Los Angeles.

CSH BEST OF

CSH #7 WILLI HILBERT

CSH #11 ANGELINA SCHITIK

CSH #16A TEUTA QELAJ

CSH #21 ALEXANDER SIEGFRIED

CSH #23A SARA HEIDE

CSH #25 STEPHANIE DICK / JULIANE VON GRADOWSKI

CSH VS. BIM

CSH VS. **BIM**

Building Information Modeling (BIM) stands for a digital planning methodology that interlinks all processes related to design, planning, construction and operation of a building. All information is recorded in a database and is associatively connected via parametric links. In addition to graphic information about the building geometry, this includes non-graphic information such as quantities, materials, energy consumption and cost estimation. One of the major benefits of using BIM is an improvement of the planning process in terms of planning quality. Using a common, continuously synchronized set of data records and the immediate availability of all current and relevant data result in significantly improved information exchange between the planning team members.

Dana K. Smith, Director of the buildingSMART alliance puts it like this: "The concept of BIM is to build a building virtually, prior to building it physically, in order to work out problems, and simulate and analyze potential impacts". Thus, even during the early planning phases, an evaluation of the performance can offer important information for the future operation of the building. As a result, this not only leads to optimized planning processes but also aims at an optimized and sustainable architecture.

The connection to the Case Study Houses that suggests itself is the objective which then and now has always focused on creating an efficient, fast and low-cost architecture which is the promise of the BIM methods used today. With this in mind we took another look at the houses in a follow-up seminar where we integrated in the model not only the description of the 3D geometry but also specific data related to the various components. The enrichment of the model with more information can be used to gain useful insights on the various levels, such as the architectural drawings with floor plan, section and elevation, also the databases for the building components and the simulation of energy demands.

Pierre Koenig's Stahl house also serves in the following to give a better picture of BIM planning processes and to demonstrate the results.

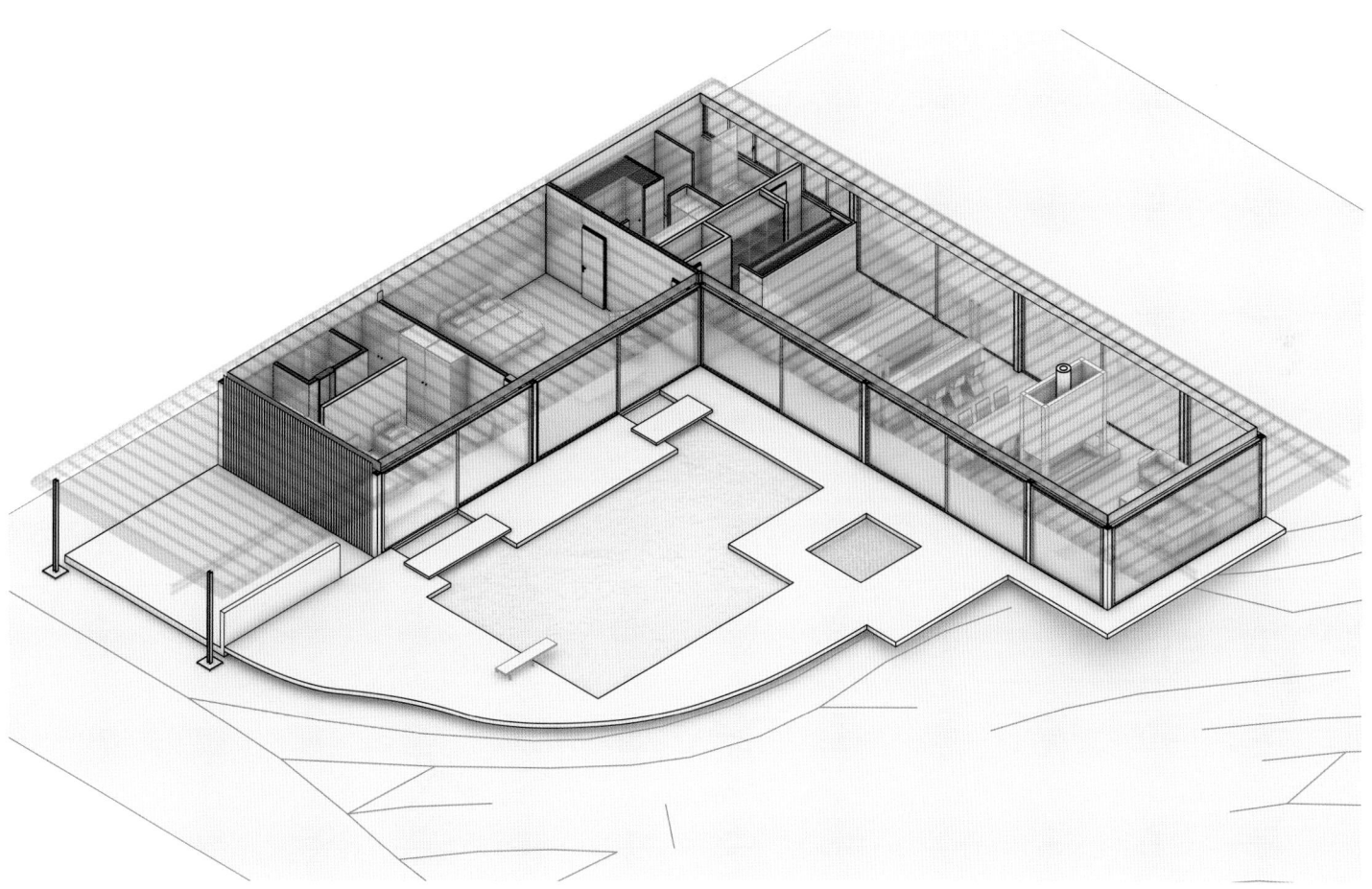

FLOORPLAN

SECTION A-A

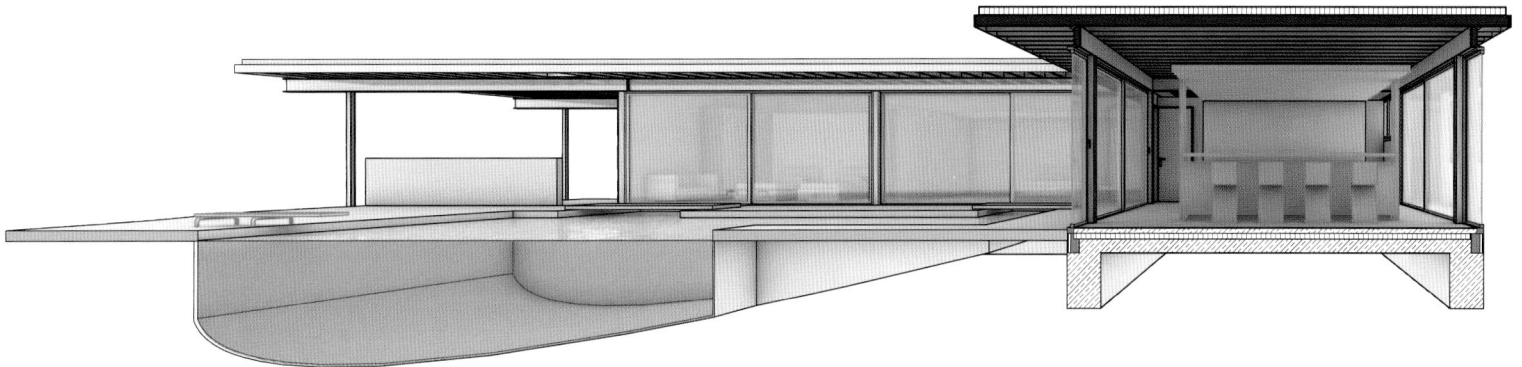

BUILDING DATA

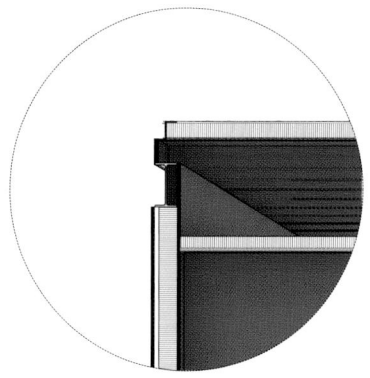

ROOM LIST

NUMBER	NAME	PERIMETER (m)	NET AREA (sqm)	FLOOR	WALL	CEILING
1	CHILDREN'S BEDROOM	26,03	30,58	CAST STONE/RUG	PLASTER	CORRUGATED METAL
2	CHILDREN'S BATHROOM	6,49	2,49	GLAZED TILES	GLAZED TILES	CORRUGATED METAL
3	MASTER BEDROOM	24,30	36,83	CAST STONE/RUG	PLASTER	CORRUGATED METAL
4	DRESSING ROOM	19,19	11,18	CAST STONE/RUG	PLASTER	SUSPENDED CEILING
5	MASTER BATHROOM	16,18	10,68	GLAZED TILES	GLAZED TILES	SUSPENDED CEILING
6	GUEST TOILET	5,58	1,63	GLAZED TILES	GLAZED TILES	SUSPENDED CEILING
7	SERVICE PORCH	19,69	12,79	CAST STONE	PLASTER	CORRUGATED METAL
8	KITCHEN AREA	26,21	33,78	CAST STONE	GLASS (PLYWOOD)	SUSPENDED CEILING
9	LIVING ROOM	30,40	54,52	CAST STONE	GLASS (METAL/PLASTER)	CORRUGATED METAL
	TOTAL	**42376,00**	**194,48**			

QUANTITY SURVEY

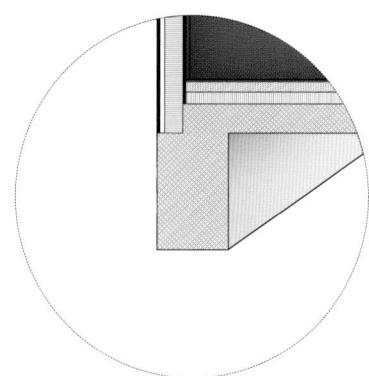

NUMBER	NAME	MATERIAL	LENGTH (m)	SURFACE (sqm)	VOLUME (cbm)	WEIGHT (kg)
1	EXCAVATION	EARTH			232,20	
2	TERRACE	CONCRETE		161,80	26,85	
3	POOL	WATER			91,97	
4	FOUNDATION	REINFORCED CONCRETE	83,65		32,17	
5	FOUNDATION SLAB	REINFORCED CONCRETE		200,54	40,11	
6	EXTERIOR WALLS	INSULATING GLASS	54,92	135,16	2,70	
7	EXTERIOR WALLS	CORRUGATED METAL	30,40	85,41	15,14	
8	INTERIOR WALLS	METAL STUD SYSTEM	12,61	32,30	3,23	
9	INTERIOR WALLS	GYPSUM BOARD	29,94	66,64	10,00	
10	COLUMNS	WF STEEL PROFILES	47,36		0,10	794,87
11	ROOF STRUCTURE	WF STEEL PROFILES	105,02		0,57	4446,55
12	ROOF CLADDING	CORRUGATED METAL		330,00		

SECTION B-B

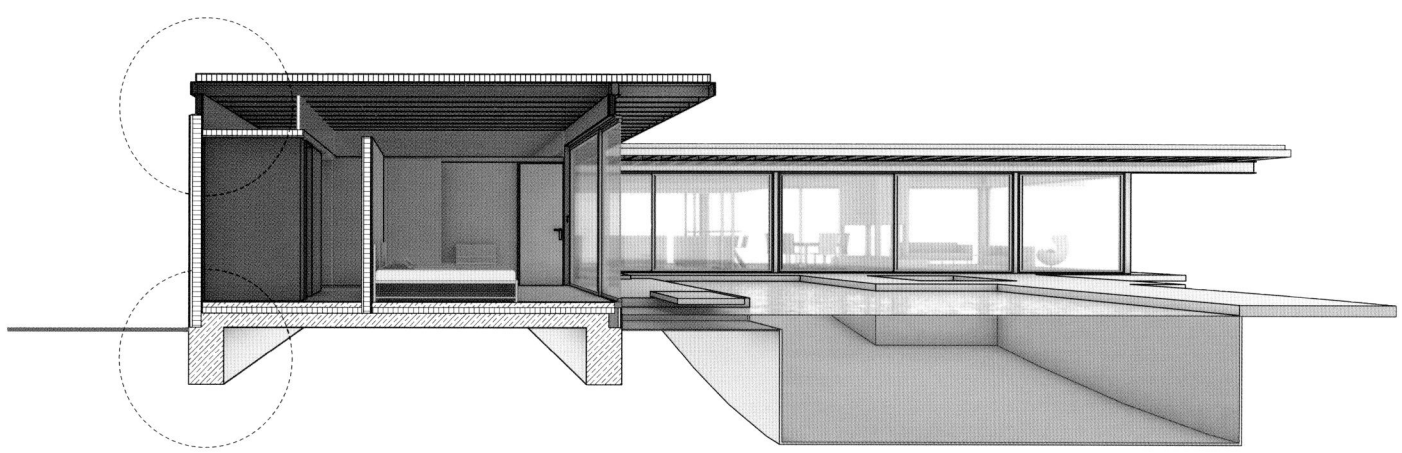

ELEVATION SOUTH & EAST

ELEVATION NORTH & WEST

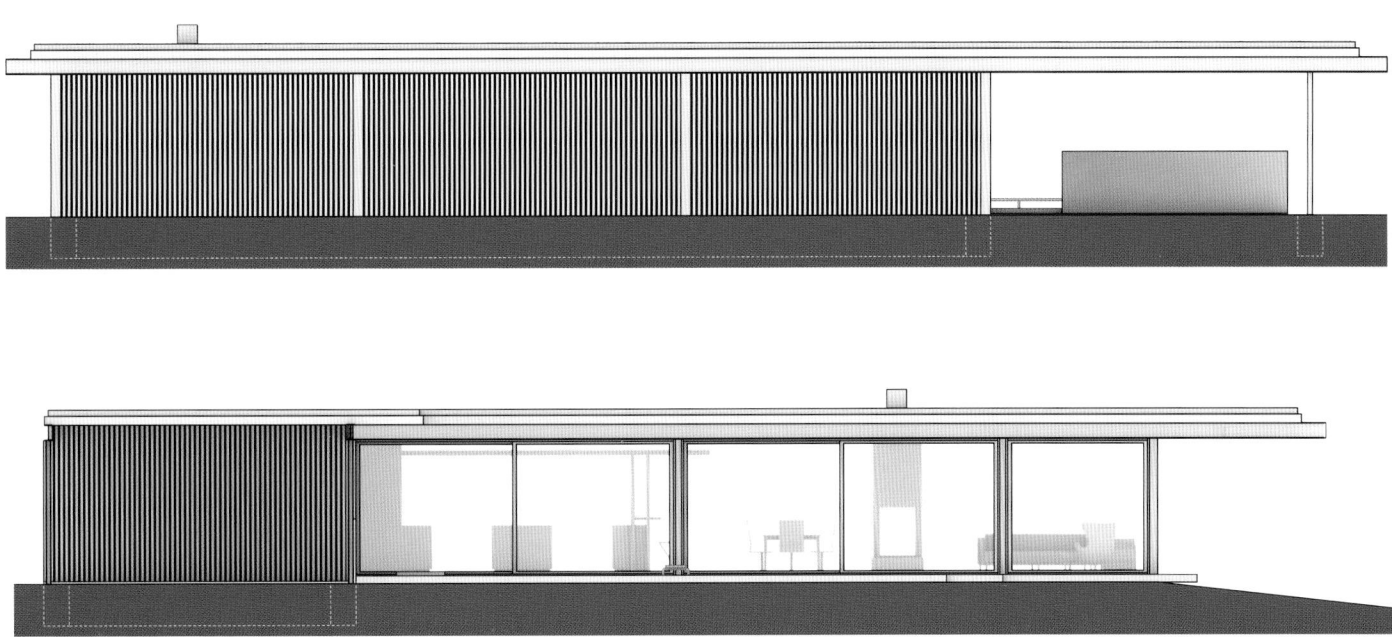

CONSTRUCTION DOCUMENTATION

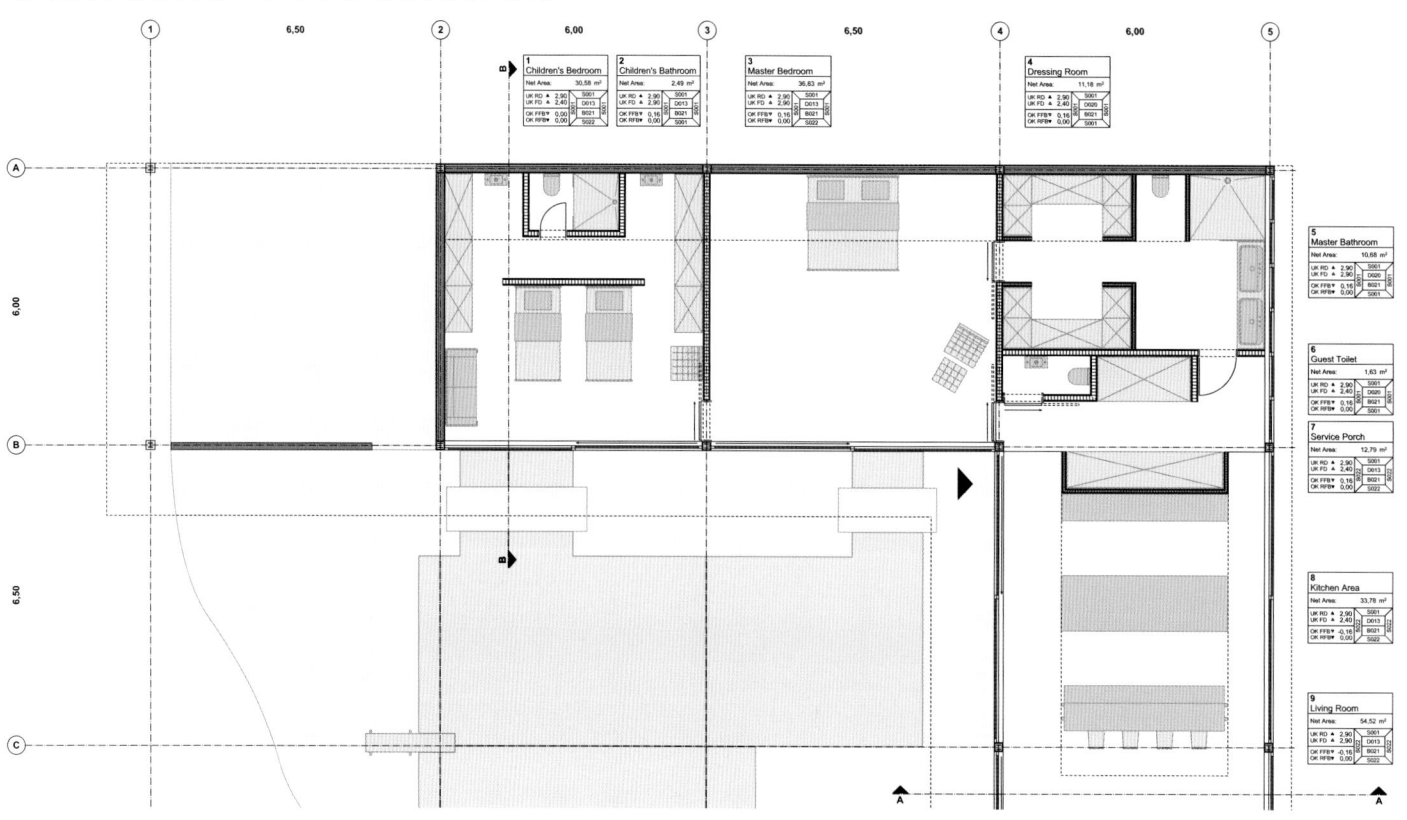

IFC DATA

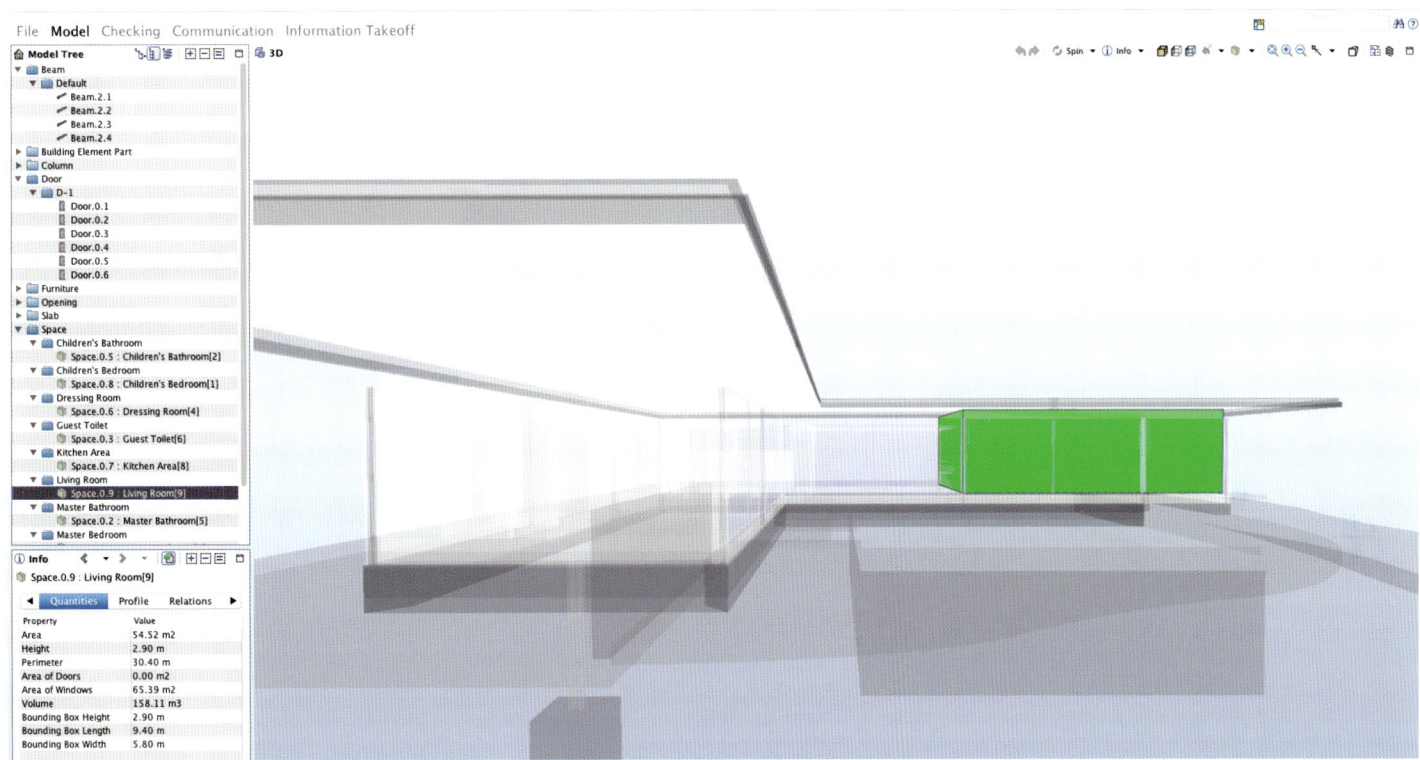

APPENDIX

ABOUT THE AUTHORS

Marco Hemmerling teaches and conducts research as Professor of Computational Design in Architecture at the Cologne University of Technology, Arts and Sciences and is director of the post-graduate Master program Computational Design and Construction at the East-Westphalia University of Applied Sciences. Previously he was Professor at the Detmold School of Architecture and Interior Architecture as well as Visiting Professor at the Polytechnic University in Milan.

Markus Graf is a Research Assistant in the Department of Computer Aided Design at the Detmold School of Architecture and Interior Architecture. As an architect, he has gained extensive experience in the application of Building Information Modeling. Markus also provides consulting services for architectural offices and companies dealing with integrated building planning and digital planning tools.

Uta Pottgiesser is Dean of the Detmold School of Architecture and Interior Architecture. She holds the Chair for Building Construction and Materials and is directing the master program International Facade Design and Construction. She is Secretary of the Docomomo International Scientific Committee of Technology and was a visiting researcher at the Getty Conservation Institute in Los Angeles.

AKNOWLEDGMENTS

The works presented in this book were created in the Bachelor course ´Computer Aided Design', between 2013 and 2015 at the Detmold School of Architecture and Interior Architecture, East-Westphalia University of Applied Sciences, under the direction of Prof. Marco Hemmerling and Markus Graf.

A very special thank you goes to Maja Rokohl for her active collaboration on the publication and Martin Tintelott for the preparation of individual visualizations; we would also like to thank all student assistants and students who participated and contributed to the success of the seminars. Thanks also to Ruth Deans for her professional translation.

Many of the 3D-models of the digitally remastered Case Study Houses are available for download at www.vectorworks.de/case-study-houses.

The visuals were produced as part of the course work with the following CAD applications: Vectorworks, Cinema4D, Photoshop.

The publication was made possible with the friendly support of Vectorworks Inc. and ComputerWorks.
.

STUDENT ASSITANTS

Benedikt Aumann, Tobias Brehm, Catalin Bruns, Viktoria Butin, Swantje Dargel, Larissa Deutsch, Stephanie Dick, Juliane von Gradowski, Lydia Jochim, Michael Knieper, Alexandra Kötz, Timon Mäder, James Martens, Inna Metche, Faina Pauls, Jens Renneke, Maja Rokohl, Eike Scheps ,Timo Schröder, Alexander Siegfried, Dennis Suckau, Roman Thielemann, Martin Tintelott, Pascal Völz, Robert Vortkamp

LITERATURE

Esther McCoy; Modern California Houses - Case Study Houses 1945-1962, Reinhold, 1962; reissued as „Case Study Houses 1945-1962" by Hennessey & Ingalls, 1977.

Mike Davis: City of Quartz - Excavating the Future in Los Angeles, Verso Publishers, 1990

Elizabeth A. T. Smith, Peter Gössel, Julius Shulman; Case Study Houses – The complete CSH-Program 1945-1966, Taschen, Cologne 2001

Ethel Buisson, Thomas Billard; Presence of the Case Study Houses, Birkhäuser, Basel 2004

Elizabeth A.T. Smith; Case Study Houses, Taschen, Cologne 2006

David F. Travers, Nina Wiener (ed.); Arts & Architecture 1945-54: The Complete Reprint, Taschen, Cologne 2008

Marco Hemmerling, Anke Tiggemann: Digital Design Manual, DOM Publishers, Berlin 2011

TABLE OF FIGURES

VECTORWORKS ARCHITEKTUR

AUTHORIZED DISTRIBUTOR

Holzer Kobler Architekturen. Rendering LMcad ArchViz Studio

YOU SEE THE WORLD DIFFERENTLY. TRANSFORM IT.

www.vectorworks-campus.eu